# FATHERS & TODDLERS

# OTHER BOOKS WRITTEN
# BY JEAN MARZOLLO
# AND ILLUSTRATED BY
# IRENE TRIVAS

## *For Parents*

*Fathers & Babies:*
*How Babies Grow and What They Need from You,*
*from Birth to 18 Months*

*The New Kindergarten*

*Birthday Parties for Children*

*Superkids*

*Supertot*

*Learning Through Play*
(coauthored with Janice Lloyd)


## *For Children*

*My First Book of Biographies*

*39 Kids on the Block series*

*The House That Dreams Painted*

# FATHERS & TODDLERS

## How Toddlers Grow and What They Need from You from 18 Months to Three Years

JEAN MARZOLLO
ILLUSTRATED BY IRENE TRIVAS

HarperPerennial
*A Division of* HarperCollins*Publishers*

HarperCollins books may be purchased for educational, business, or sales promotional use. For information please write: Special Markets Department, HarperCollins Publishers, Inc., 10 East 53rd Street, New York, NY 10022.

FIRST EDITION

Library of Congress Cataloging-in-Publication Data

Marzollo, Jean.
    Fathers & toddlers : how toddlers grow and what they need from you from 18 months to three years / Jean Marzollo ; illustrated by Irene Trivas. — 1st ed.
        p.   cm.
        ISBN 0-06-096907-5
        1. Toddlers.   2. Father and child.   3. Toddlers—Psychology.   4. Child rearing   I. Trivas, Irene.
II. Title.   III. Title: Fathers and toddlers.
HQ774.5.M36   1994
649'.123—dc20                                    94-8246

94 95 96 97 98 ❖/RRD 10 9 8 7 6 5 4 3 2 1

FOR KRISTIN, BARRY, JAMIE & KATHARINE
O'CONNELL
J.M.

FOR NIELS DE TERRA
I.T.

WITH SPECIAL THANKS TO:

Ellen Gambino and Katherine Martin Widmer

# CONTENTS

# INTRODUCTION: FATHERS & TODDLERS

*Fathers & Toddlers* is a guide for fathers who would like to help and enjoy their toddlers fully. Toddlers aren't infants anymore. You can't just feed them a bottle and hope they'll fall asleep in your arms. Toddlers run around, open doors, and climb on furniture. They can be messy and feisty. They don't necessarily play what you want to play or sit quietly when you want them to. They can be great, but they have their impossible moments, and at that time they require a lot of understanding.

This book is for all kinds of fathers: fathers who help to take care of their children in the evening and on weekends and fathers who take care of their children full-time at home. (For that matter, it's for mothers and baby-sitters, too. The advice in this book is for anyone and everyone who cares for children between the ages of 18 months and three years.)

**The problems of the evening and weekend dad.**

In some ways, it's harder for the father who works away from home and sees his child in the evening and on weekends. He doesn't get enough time to learn how to deal with toddlers. Such a father is often baffled or miffed by them. To deal with such feelings, some dads try to avoid parenting jobs by being too busy with other tasks, by not being around at all, or by using the not-my-problem and the I-don't-know-how strategies.

**The not-my-problem and the I-don't-know-how strategies.**

The not-my-problem strategy is when Dad notices a problem involving the toddler and *tells* the mother about it, the assumption being that it's not Dad's responsibility. The I-don't-know-how strategy is when Dad says he would like to help but can't because he doesn't know how. These strategies cause more problems than they solve. The toddler's problem is still there, and now Mom is annoyed. The bottom line is: mothers need help with child care, and fathers are smart to learn when to deliver and how to deliver—without complaining. Such skills may be partly instinctive, but mostly they are learned by trial and error. Hopefully, this guidebook will help you avoid many errors.

Now, nobody said that the job of taking care of toddlers is easy. It's not. Toddlers challenge one's imagination, patience, practicality, ability to plan, ability to recoup, and sense of humor.

**The hard parts of being with toddlers.**

You may feel frustration, the like of which you've never felt before, and anger that can make you feel violent. But you weather these storms for the sake of your child, who is trying to grow and needs your deepest understanding.

**The easy parts of being with a toddler.**

Toddlers are not always impossible. They can be adorable and charming. They don't always feel like being sloppy, whiney, clingy, annoying, and loud. Sometimes they scream in the market, and other times they'll ride in your cart being as well mannered as you could ever hope for. Toddlers can be sensitive to your feelings and anxious to help you. They want to sense the organization of the world and want to be a part of it.

**The secret to understanding toddlers.**

Toddlers have a craving to learn and a natural ability to teach themselves. Unfortunately, what they don't have is sufficient knowledge of the world to keep themselves out of danger. You are their caretaker. The secret of caring for toddlers is to set up situations in which they can exercise their independent and curious minds.

The chapters in this book are organized by age group, but please don't take them too seriously. Basically, the age groups are there to help you plug into your child's level; but anything you find in an earlier chapter you should feel free to do later, and anything you find in a later chapter, you should feel free to try earlier, perhaps in a modified way. Singing, humming, and scatting, for example, are recommended on page 39, but please indulge your child with your musical performances whenever you are inspired.

*Fathers & Toddlers* is your guide to use as you like. Read it front to back or back to front—whatever works to help you enjoy your toddler and helps your toddler enjoy you.

# CHAPTER ONE:
## 18 TO 20 MONTHS

A one-and-a-half-year-old child gives you the opportunity to go back to your childhood and play. If anyone asks you what you are doing when you're on the floor acting like a growling tiger, just say that you're preparing your child for college. For the fact is, children do learn through play. Play is the activity that they invent to study the world around them.

Some learning psychologists have estimated that by the age of five, a child's intelligence quotient (IQ) is basically established. They say that by this age attitudes toward learning and patterns of thinking have settled into children's minds, and that these same attitudes and patterns guide their thoughts for the rest of their lives. Fortunately, the way children learn is fun, fun for them and potentially fun for you. By understanding that through play children learn to concentrate, exercise their imagination, try out ideas, and practice various behaviors, you may come to respect the process enough to get involved with it.

*Approximate age range: 18 to 20 months*

Your involvement and interest in your child's play will make a big difference in your child's life. In homes where discovery is discouraged, children often learn how not to play, a tragic outcome, to say the least. In homes where early explorations are encouraged, the minds and personalities of children grow and develop the potential that is each child's natural legacy.

Your child's spirit is a mixture of curiosity and pleasure. But, once you let it start to grow on you to the point where you truly enjoy playing with your child, you may feel betrayed. You offer a favorite food or activity and your child shouts, "No!" Suddenly, your child is no fun at all. Why? What's going on? This chapter and later chapters as well will explain what your toddler is going through and tell you ways to cope.

*Approximate age range: 18 to 20 months*

# RUNNING (AWKWARDLY)

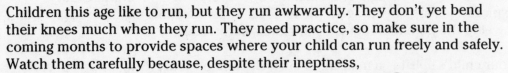

Children this age like to run, but they run awkwardly. They don't yet bend their knees much when they run. They need practice, so make sure in the coming months to provide spaces where your child can run freely and safely. Watch them carefully because, despite their ineptness, they are brave and adventurous—and surprisingly fast. So watch out! Toddlers can start to run across the street while your head is turned to chat with a friend.

Children learning to run inevitably fall down. Since they don't have far to go, they usually don't get hurt seriously. Bloody lips generally heal quickly. React calmly, but don't be afraid to consult a doctor if you think it's necessary.

*Approximate age range: 18 to 20 months*

# PULLING AND PUSHING THINGS

Children this age also like to demonstrate their ability to walk well and to make something else move, too. That's why they like wheel toys they can pull along after them and toys they can push ahead of them.

Pull toys and push toys come in various shapes and sizes. Some make noises, which makes the event even more satisfying because your child is causing the noise to happen. Some toys can be both pushed and pulled.

**Pull and push toys make great presents for kids this age.**

Some of the most fun pull toys are:

• Small wagons that are not too heavy for a young child to pull

• Dogs that bark

• Other animals, such as giant caterpillars

Some of the most fun push toys are:

• See-through toys with balls inside that make sounds when they pop around

• Toy vacuum cleaners

• Toy lawn mowers

The last two can be used by your child to "help" you work.

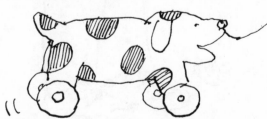

*Approximate age range: 18 to 20 months*

# THROWING THINGS

Toddlers like to hurl things. Again, this skill demonstrates to the world that they can move things and make things happen. Toddlers are not passive; they want to affect the world around them. Throwing things is one way to do that. Unfortunately, toddlers don't have very good aim, and objects they hurl are apt to go in any direction. So toddlers need to be helped to know what to throw and what not to throw—and where to throw the things they can throw.

You can help them practice throwing by giving toddlers safe things to throw. Beanbags are great, and sometimes you can get older siblings to make them as presents for toddlers. But if you don't have beanbags, make balls of tightly crumpled junk mail; your child may like to make paper balls, too. Without too much trouble, your throwing activity can turn into a clean-up game, especially after parties.

*Approximate age range: 18 to 20 months*

# WALKING UPSTAIRS

Stairs present a fascinating challenge to children. They see older people climbing up and down them, and they want to try, too. They start by crawling up and down, gradually progressing to walking up and down. At first they put both feet on a tread, take one step, and move the other foot up so that they have both feet on the next tread. They start this process when they are ready, and they need you to hold their hand. By 21 months they have usually mastered the two-feet-to-a-tread method.

**Gates.**

Gates are necessary at both the top and the bottom of stairs. Install them well, and make sure your child can't open them. Gates are very important in preventing staircase accidents.

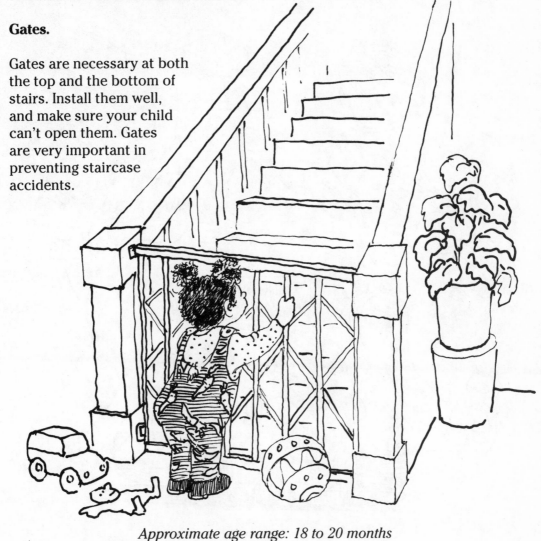

*Approximate age range: 18 to 20 months*

# LISTENING TO MUSIC

Toddlers benefit from hearing music, experiencing rhythms, and, most of all, from sharing the numerous sensory pleasures of music with you. To have a musical child, you don't have to be professional musicians nor is it necessary to send your toddler off to piano lessons. If you want your child to enjoy music, start by enjoying it together as a family at home. Sing your favorite songs to your child, listen together to children's tapes and CDs, and have family jam sessions with maracas, drums, and tambourines.

*Approximate age range: 18 to 20 months*

# DANCING TO MUSIC

Toddlers like to dance in different ways. Sometimes they like to stand in place and jiggle. Other times they like to walk around to music. They also like to dance with you, either holding your hands or being waltzed around the room in your arms. Dancing is good for kids. It helps them learn about music, develop coordination, feel creative, and have fun.

**Different dance activities:**

**Mirror dancing.**

Dance and sing together in front of a full-length mirror. Your toddler likes to see the two of you having a good time.

**Musical toy game.**

Save a musical crib toy for dancing to. Let your child hold it and make it go. When the music plays, you both dance. When the music stops, you both stop dancing.

**Exercise dance.**

Make up a series of simple exercises that are good for you and simple enough for your child to more or less do with you. The simpler the dance, the better. A five-minute routine is about all most toddlers can handle. If you want, wear weights to increase your challenge. If your child wants to wear "weights," too, put stretchy (but not tight) ponytail ties around his or her arms and legs.

*Approximate age range: 18 to 20 months*

# FINDING THINGS . . .

Here's a simple activity that helps your child practice a number of important skills. The activity consists of your asking your child to fetch a particular item, waiting for your child to find it, and rewarding your child with an enthusiastic hug when the item is brought to you. The fetching game can be played anywhere, and it doesn't require any particular equipment.

Because this activity is so basic, its multiple benefits can be overlooked, yet they bear discussion. Some of the skills this activity teaches are:

**Language skills.**

To find something you ask for requires that your child first of all understand its name. Your child may not be able to say the name but understands the meaning of the word when you say it. Your child is learning to react to a request and to understand directions.

**Social skills.**

Your child is learning to cooperate by bringing you something you ask for.

**Gross motor and fine motor skills.**

Gross motor skills involve large muscles such as arm and leg muscles. Fine motor skills involve small muscles, such as hand muscles. Finding things and bringing them to you can involve both.

**Task persistence.**

To start a job and finish it is one of the most useful skills a person can learn. The task you ask for should be simple enough for your child to do.

*Approximate age range: 18 to 20 months*

# . . . And Bringing Them To You

Listen to all the language that your child hears when you play this game. Such language enriches your child's life and is one of the greatest gifts you give your child.

**Listen . . .**

*Where's Rabbit? Is she hiding? Can you find her? Will you bring her to me, please? Is she under your crib? No? Is she peeking out from behind the chair? No? Is she under the pillow on the couch? Yes? Is that her ear you see? You found Rabbit! That's my girl. Now, will you please bring Rabbit to me? Thank you. What a good job! You want me to hide Rabbit again?*

Hint: Only hide things that your child will be able to find. For younger children, put the object across the room in a place that's easy for your child to spot. Your child will be excited to "find" it there.

*Approximate age range: 18 to 20 months*

# MAKE A TOWER OF 3 TO 4 BLOCKS

The main guideline to keep in mind when helping your child play with blocks is that toddlers need blocks they can lift by themselves. One-and-a-half-year-olds are not yet ready for heavy wooden blocks. They like the small lightweight plastic or wooden blocks. They also like bigger hollow cardboard blocks, especially if you lend your assistance in making a tower. Don't get too elaborate with your plans. Children this age usually make towers that are only three or four blocks tall. For them, this is a major accomplishment. For you, it's a time to appreciate just how much eye-hand coordination your child has acquired in a year and a half.

*Approximate age range: 18 to 20 months*

# KNOCK IT OVER

The fun of making a tower isn't fully realized until it is knocked over. Young children delight in being able to feel powerful. After they knock the tower over, they want to build it again. Building and knocking over towers is a good activity that you can enjoy as long as you don't have to keep on picking up the blocks. If your child wants to build and destroy block towers, set him or her on the floor. If you feel like it, count blocks as they are added to the tower, and make appropriate comments such as "Boom!" as your child topples them.

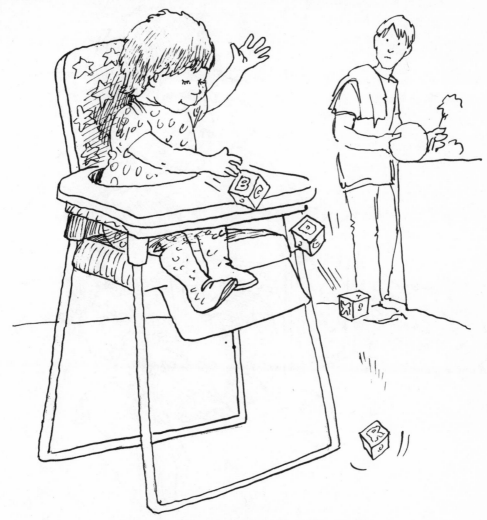

*Approximate age range: 18 to 20 months*

# "TURN THE PAGE"

Toddlers like to sit on your lap and have you read to them. Not only do they like to look at the pictures and hear your voice, but they also like other aspects of book reading. For example, they are intrigued by the action of page turning. When your child reaches out to help you turn a page, respond positively. Let your child turn the page with you, or let the child turn the page alone, if possible. Eventually, when it's time to turn a page, you can just say, "Turn the page," and your proud child may do it for you.

*Approximate age range: 18 to 20 months*

# PICTURE BOOKS FOR ONE-AND-A-HALF-YEAR-OLDS

Your library and bookstore clerk can recommend many good books, but in the meantime, here are some terrific ones to read to your toddler at bedtime, naptime, or any other quiet time of the day:

*Richard Scarry's Best Word Book Ever*
  by Richard Scarry
*Charlie Parker Played Be Bop*
  by Chris Raschka
*The Very Hungry Caterpillar*
  by Eric Carle
*Good Night Moon*
  by Margaret Wise Brown
*The Little Fireman*
  by Margaret Wise Brown
*The Carrot Seed*
  by Ruth Krauss
*Bright Eyes,*
*Brown Skin*
  by Cheryl Willis
  Hudson and
  Bernette G. Ford
*More, More, More,*
*Said the Baby*
  by Vera B.
  Williams

*Approximate age range: 18 to 20 months*

# LITTLE THINGS & CONTAINERS

One-and-a-half-year-olds enjoy handling small objects. They like to manipulate these objects in different ways and will think up things to do with the objects by themselves, occasionally taking suggestions from you. Sometimes kids will vary their activities; other times they'll do the same activity over and over again with satisfaction. If your child seems bored, introduce a new container to explore. Get your child to pick up the small things with you as a game when finished with them. The last container used can be the storage container.

**Little things kids like.**

Stones and pebbles

Acorns and nuts

Small cars

Small people and animal figures

**Interesting containers.**

Boxes of all sizes

Clean plastic bottles that little things can be dropped into

Empty pill bottles—cap them and shake little things inside

Mailing tubes—what happens when you drop things inside?

**Safety precautions.**

Don't give young children toys that are so small they could be swallowed, unless you are playing *with* your child and are watching to make sure your child does not suck on them.

*Approximate age range: 18 to 20 months*

FILL UP A MUFFIN TIN WITH PEBBLES

POUR NUTS INTO A BOX AND TAKE THEM OUT AGAIN

MAKE A "TRAIN" OUT OF STONES

POKE STONES INTO A SMALL HOLE CUT IN A CARDBOARD BOX

FILL A PIE PLATE WITH ACORNS

*Approximate age range: 18 to 20 months*

# THIS IS TOO HARD FOR ME!

**What does "developmentally appropriate" mean?**

"Developmentally appropriate" is a term used by educators to refer to materials and activities that suit your child's abilities—not your child's age, because children of the same age may have different abilities. Developmentally appropriate materials are neither too hard nor too easy for your child, but appropriately challenging, and therefore quite satisfying, both to your child and to you as well, because you don't have to do the activity for your child.

*Approximate age range: 18 to 20 months*

# THIS IS TOO EASY!

**How can I tell what is developmentally appropriate for my child?**

Observe your child at play. Which toys does your child really like to play with? Which activities and games capture your child's attention? These are the toys and activities that are developmentally appropriate for your child. The toys and games described in this book can steer you in the right direction, but the best guide is your child, who wants to be neither bored nor frustrated.

*Approximate age range: 18 to 20 months*

# SITTING IN A CHAIR THAT FITS

**This chair is too high.**

**This chair is too low.**

**These chairs are just right.**

If you want your child to eat calmly or work quietly at activities such as coloring and putting puzzles together, you would do well to think about where you are asking your child to sit. Chairs that are too high or too low for the table are uncomfortable for children, and they may be unsafe, too. Children sit longer when they are comfortable.

The two most comfortable chairs for children are high chairs and toddler-size chairs that fit toddler-size desks. You can buy inexpensive plastic child-size furniture; it is a good investment because a comfortable child is a contented child. Also, low chairs and desks are safer than high chairs.

*Approximate age range: 18 to 20 months*

# FEEDING ONESELF

**Learning to use a spoon and a cup.**

Children this age want to learn to use a spoon. Serve them foods, such as mashed potatoes and mashed beans, that will stay on the spoon. Don't expect your child to get all the food into his or her mouth. Be prepared to clean up messes calmly as learning proceeds. To help your child learn to use a cup, provide a training cup with handles, a weighted bottom to prevent tipping, and possibly a cap with a built-in straw.

**Favorite finger foods.**

Toddlers like to eat food they can pick up with their fingers. Make sure their hands are clean first, then serve them a plate of tidbits, such as: cheese cubes, vegetable cubes, fruit slices, berries, tofu cubes, sliced hot dogs (nutritious type), cubes of meat, strips of French toast, and bite-size pieces of omelet.

*Approximate age range: 18 to 20 months*

# STUBBORNNESS

One-and-a-half-year-olds begin to exhibit a sense of possessiveness. They start to perceive things, such as favorite books and toys, as belonging to them. This development is part of a natural and healthy growth in self-awareness.

A child needs to learn that these are my pajamas and those are yours, that this is my shoe and that is yours. This sense of possessiveness will lead eventually to a sense of respect for other people's possessions.

But feelings of possessiveness are complicated. Children want to wear a sibling's socks, despite the sibling's admonitions. They may also want to possess another child's toy.

**Be creative.**

In these situations, think of something else your child might like to have. Offer it enticingly. Distraction is an effective strategy with toddlers.

**Be loose.**

Keep your sense of humor, and don't let your child intimidate you.

**Be flexible.**

Socks? Who cares? Is it really worth a fight? Maybe the sibling will relent.

*Approximate age range: 18 to 20 months*

# TANTRUMS

Toddlers occasionally have temper tantrums. They usually happen when they get a little older, but sometimes they happen at this age, too, and even at younger ages. A temper tantrum is when a child screams and hollers and kicks and flails out and won't respond to any effort on your part to calm him or her down.

**Other parents experience them, too.**

Temper tantrums are embarrassing, but not for your child. Your child doesn't care what anyone thinks. They are embarrassing for you because suddenly it appears that you have raised the most beastly child in the whole wide world. When and if your child has a temper tantrum, accept your embarrassment and then get past it. Anyone watching who has a child is probably sympathizing with you. As for those others who are watching critically and thinking that you are a wretched parent, ignore them.

**What to do?**

Don't try to argue or reason now. If you have to finish up business in a store, do so as quickly as possible. Make sure your child is safe. Do not hit your child. It's harmful and will only make your child cry more.

If you are dropping your child off at a day-care center or at a baby-sitter's home, take your cues from the caregiver. If she says it's okay to leave, leave. Caregivers are good at handling upset children, and the truth is, most children calm down after their parents leave.

Tell yourself that this, too, shall pass. And it will. Children outgrow temper tantrums once they develop a sense of how the world is looking at them. They really do become more civilized in expressing their feelings.

*Approximate age range: 18 to 20 months*

# Pointing and Naming

One of the first things that children learn to point to and name are their body parts. Simple games involving this activity are enjoyed immensely by toddlers, and it is great for showing off to visitors, especially gleeful grandparents.

**Pointing and Naming 101.**

The game goes like this: You say, "Where's your nose?" And your child points to it. Stick to basic facial features: eyes, nose, mouth.

**Pointing and Naming 102.**

You say: "Where's Daddy's nose?" And your child points to your nose. And so on, to Mommy's nose and Grandma's nose.

**Pointing and Naming 103.**

Add other body parts: ears, hair, cheek. Elbow is a funny one.

**Pointing and Naming 104.**

Eventually your child says, "Nose," or a word that sounds like "nose." This is graduate-level activity and very impressive. Pointing is one thing, but naming—wow!

*Approximate age range: 18 to 20 months*

# BODY PARTS & SELF-AWARENESS

I LOVE YOUR EYES
I LOVE YOUR NOSE
I LOVE YOUR TUMMY
I LOVE YOUR TOES!

Some parents think learning is something that happens in the brain only. They think books and educational toys are the key to unlocking the treasures of the brain. While books and toys are thrilling indeed, they are only part of the way a child perceives the world. Learning for children involves the whole body: eyes, ears, mouths, teeth, hands, feet, tummies, arms, and legs.

Children start learning about their bodies at a very young age, and they learn from you. Convey respect and delight for your child's body. Teach your child that bodies need to be well cared for, exercised, and appreciated. Your positive attitude about your child's body will help your child develop a positive sense of self-awareness.

*Approximate age range: 18 to 20 months*

# CHANGING TABLE GAMES

BOO!

The changing table is a great place to play affectionate games with your child. Keep some toys handy for your child to play with, in case you're not in the mood for games. But if you are, here are some you and your child might enjoy.

• **Peek-a-Boo.**

It's a babyish game, but kids enjoy it for a long, long time.

• **This Little Piggy.**

You say the rhyme while you wiggle your baby's toes and then tickle your child under the chin.

• **Naming Body Parts.**

You ask your child to point to his nose and so on. See page 37 for more information.

• **What Does a Cow Say?**

In the straight version of this game, your child gives the correct answer, "Moo." In the silly version, he or she gives a deliberately wrong answer, such as "Meow." Hilarious for toddlers!

*Approximate age range: 18 to 20 months*

# HUMMING, SINGING, AND SCATTING

Children this age are beginning to hum and sing. The inception of these interesting skills often escapes parental attention. But when you think about it, babies aren't born knowing how to hum and sing. They learn these skills now, especially if you hum and sing to them. What? You don't have a good voice? Oh, yes, you do. According to your child, you are Pavarotti.

Scatting is useful if you can't remember words to songs. Scatting is singing nonsense syllables. If you like, take the words and sounds your toddler likes and make up a scatting song for them. This is fun to do while you're changing your child's diaper. *Baby, Baby, be-bop, ba-dee-bop!*

*Approximate age range: 18 to 20 months*

# LEARNING TO USE SPEECH

Children want to learn to talk. Sometimes you can see them practicing talking with each other. Even if the sounds they are making don't sound exactly right, they seem to have all the gestures of adults. They like to say "Sh-h-h" and "No" and "Hi" to each other with all the hand movements that they see you use. They are learning, learning, learning all the time they talk.

*Approximate age range: 18 to 20 months*

# A VOCABULARY OF 10 TO 12 WORDS

A magic moment occurs when your child names a new familiar object for the first time. Being able verbally to make the connection between the spoken word and the actual object is a giant step for your child. The process of language acquisition is truly amazing, and watching it happen is one of the great joys of parenthood. What can you do to assist? Talk with your child in natural, joyful ways; and show your respect and appreciation for what your child is accomplishing. Soon you'll be able to talk together. True, you may only have five shared words at this point, but the list will grow . . . rapidly.

*Approximate age range: 18 to 20 months*

# THE COMMANDER GENERAL

Language acquisition brings power to children, and they soak it up. They love to be able to give orders. Their commands are blunt because their language skills are limited. They are not yet able to say, "Would you please pass me an apple?" But they can say, "Gimme dat!" By complying with the order, you enable your child to feel the power he or she wants to experience. So, if the request is reasonable, honor it. Children need to feel the power of language. If the request is unreasonable, offer a substitute. In time, you'll be able to teach your child to say please.

*Approximate age range: 18 to 20 months*

# BABY TALK

Toddlers occasionally like to talk baby talk. Sometimes they talk baby talk because they really can't pronounce a word, and sometimes they have distinct speech impediments. Most young children's speech problems straighten out as they mature. By the time they are well into elementary school, they usually can pronounce the *r*'s and *s*'s that used to give them so much trouble.

But usually toddlers who regress and talk baby talk do so because they want to. They want to remember what it was like to feel like a baby, and they want to see what reaction they get from adults when they talk baby talk. Toddlers who have new siblings figure that baby talk will get them the attention that the new baby gets.

The best way to deal with baby talk is to ignore it or even play with it in a friendly way with your child, acknowledging that you are both playing a game. In general, however, don't talk baby talk with your child. You say words normally, and accept what your child says, however he or she says it.

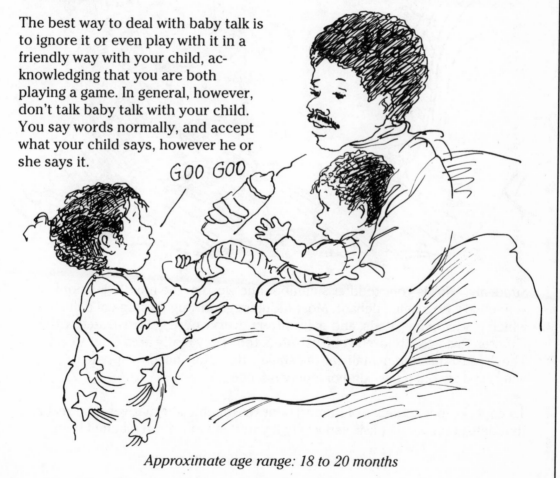

*Approximate age range: 18 to 20 months*

# MY FAVORITE NEW WORD

Suddenly, "No" is your toddler's number one word of the month. It's not just *your* child who's being defiant. Most toddlers go through a stage of defiance, which is why moms, dads, and baby-sitters everywhere get frustrated with children this age. Children get frustrated, too. They really aren't out to get you. They're just developmentally at the stage where they need to spread their wings and try out a new kind of independence.

To cope, keep your sense of humor, offer reasonable alternatives, and realize that defiant moments pass, especially if you don't make too much of them.

*Approximate age range: 18 to 20 months*

# SECURITY BLANKETS

Security blankets are those worn-out blankets that children must have in order to go to bed. Security blankets do not have to be blankets. They can be certain pacifiers, certain cuddly toys, and certain bottles. Professionals call them "attachment objects." Some children call them necessary.

### The problem with security blankets.

It's very simple. As comforting as they are—and they are—they are problems waiting to happen. The problem comes when the attachment object is not there. It was left behind at Grandma's house. Or it didn't get packed in order to go to Grandma's house and now Baby can't sleep. Or it needs to be washed, but Baby can't part with it—or rejects the cleaner version with horror.

### Prevention is the best medicine.

If your child does not have a security blanket, don't introduce one. Children don't really need these things; they just think they do. Never suggest that a child must have a particular item in order to go to sleep or to take to day care. Children can learn to go to sleep peacefully without a security blanket. They can learn to go to day care without a certain toy.

### The cure for security blankets.

Parents have come up with ingenious solutions. They have cut blankets down gradually until the child has nothing but a small square to hold. They have convinced toddlers to wrap up their security blankets and give them as a gifts to newborn children. They have offered more general substitutes—any toy instead of a particular rabbit named Fluffy. And they have been patient. College graduates do not carry security blankets. Sometimes all a parent can do is give in and wait.

*Approximate age range: 18 to 20 months*

# DISCIPLINE

Picture it: Your toddler has been playing quietly in the next room while you have been talking on the phone. You have kept an ear out for your child and have heard your child playing very contentedly. So you haven't worried about your child's safety. However, when you go to check upon your child, you discover that your child has torn off all the leaves of your prize rubber tree plant. Rage sweeps through you, and what do you do? Shouting is too scary for toddlers, and spanking only makes things worse.

First, you control your rage. If you can't, you get someone else to watch your child. Second, you try to be objective and look again at the situation. Your child really did not mean to do anything wrong. Third, you react appropriately. The best way to handle this is to give a simple explanation of what was wrong and then to give your child a hug to show forgiveness.

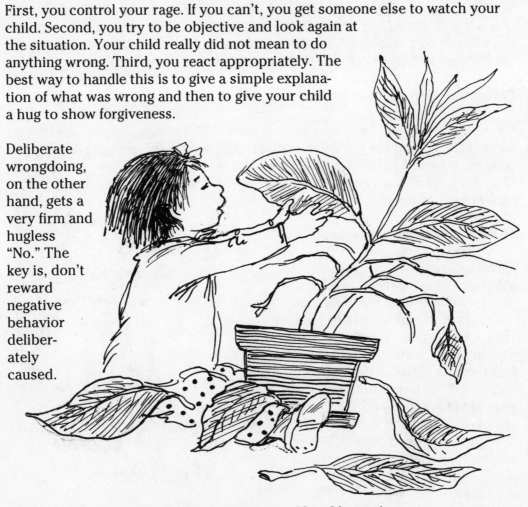

Deliberate wrongdoing, on the other hand, gets a very firm and hugless "No." The key is, don't reward negative behavior deliberately caused.

*Approximate age range: 18 to 20 months*

# LEARNING RIGHT & WRONG

Many discipline problems can be prevented by showing children the proper way to treat objects and deal with situations. After your child has destroyed your plant and you have calmed down, teach your child how to help take care of your plants. Be clear. Say, "We don't pull green leaves off plants because that destroys the plant. Sometimes we pull off old brown leaves because they are dead and the plant doesn't need them anymore." Let your child help you take off some dead leaves.

Children can perform useful tasks around the home. They like to do this. They like to be helpful. They don't really want to be "bad." It takes imagination on your part to think of little jobs children can do. You let your child do jobs, such as misting plants, with you, not because your child is really helping you. You could do the job better and faster. You let your child help you because your child needs to know how to do things right, as well as how to avoid doing things wrong.

And since misting plants is a positive behavior, you reward it with a display of your gratitude.

*Approximate age range: 18 to 20 months*

47

# TODDLERS & TEDDY BEARS

Babies are often given teddy bears as presents after they are born. But actually, little babies don't care much for teddy bears so the teddy bears are ignored for a while. Now is the time to get them down from the shelf because at this age your toddler is old enough and mature enough to develop an emotional attachment to a teddy bear.

Be sure the bear is safe and well made. The eyes and nose should be embroidered on or very securely attached. There should be no buttons to chew off and swallow. Avoid wind-up, musical teddy bears. They're not as cuddly, and any small mechanism could come out and get swallowed.

*Approximate age range: 18 to 20 months*

# TEDDY BEAR ACTIVITIES

Teddy bears are good for more than cuddling. You can dance with them, sing to them, and even toss them around a little. Small teddy bears are perfect, pre-ball objects to play with. Toss them like beanbags into big boxes or baskets. Don't make this activity harder than it should be. Toddlers can stand as close as they want to the basket. There's no competition; everyone wins at the teddy bear game! If you're smart, you can develop this activity into a cleanup game.

*Approximate age range: 18 to 20 months*

# CHAPTER TWO:
# *21 TO 23 MONTHS*

**Love and language.**

Two of the most important gifts you give your child are love and language. These gifts are intricately intertwined. Most parents who love their children talk to them, and most children whose parents talk to them grow up adept with language.

**Find it difficult to talk to toddlers?**

If you find it difficult to talk to young children, you may not be focusing on them and their interests. Stop thinking about you and your interests. See what your child is interested in, and talk about that. You don't have to talk nonstop. Some fathers (and mothers and baby-sitters) are naturally taciturn. That's okay. If you are loving, the way you talk to your child will be sufficient. You may not be as lively as your child's other caregivers, but with a twinkle of the eye and a shy smile you convey extra meaning to your child.

Some fathers (and mothers and baby-sitters) are taciturn—and cold, as well. There is no heart in the few words they speak. If you suspect you are one of these, consider your child's needs. Knowing that your child needs you for both language and love can help you warm up; such a thaw can be one of the many gifts your child gives to you. If you feel that you've talked too little to your child, don't fret about it; just start now. You still have many years ahead in which to establish a caring, verbal environment.

**Don't compare your child with other children.**

Accept the way your child talks. Children have individual rates of growth in all areas: physical, emotional, intellectual, and verbal. Pronunciation skills that come easily to one child may not come easily to another. A noncritical approach to your child's language skills will make your child more likely to want to talk to you.

*Approximate age range: 21 to 23 months*

*Approximate age range: 21 to 23 months*

# Up and Down the Stairs

Up and down, down and up—toddlers continue to want to meet the challenge of stairs. Be there for them because stairs are not safe yet. Teach toddlers to hold on to the railing if they can reach it. They may want you to hold their other hand, too, but often they don't want their hand held. They want to work things out for themselves. Let them go and stand just below to catch them if they fall. If you need a rest and your child is *very* good at going up and down, sit on the third stair and let your child go up and down—but only that far.

*Approximate age range: 21 to 23 months*

# PARENTAL COMPETITION

You're sitting in the park with other parents and watching your child in the sandbox. You notice that your child can't handle the shovel as well as another child, or can't talk as well, or can't instigate projects as well. So: not good with the hands, not articulate, not a leader. These kinds of musings are natural. Most parents have them because they care so much for their children and because they are their children's advocates. Don't feel guilty for wishing your child was better or even the best. The time to worry is when you obsess about your child's shortcomings, push your child to do more than your child is capable of doing, and, should your child be the best at something, start bragging obnoxiously. If you do the latter, don't be surprised if other parents move to another bench.

*Approximate age range: 21 to 23 months*

# BALL PLAY

Toddlers are now developing some rudimentary ball skills. If you give them balls that are big and light, they are able to squat down, grasp the ball, and stand up with the ball in their hands. That's a complicated sequence, worthy of admiration! The next step is for the children to throw the ball to you. Stand close by because toddlers can't throw far. They like to throw big light balls and also little ones, such as tennis balls.

*Approximate age range: 21 to 23 months*

# KICKING A BALL

Children this age also like to kick balls around. The ball should be big and light enough for them to move around. Toddlers will try to make the ball go in the right direction, for example, toward you. If you have a group of children at your home, you can have them stand in a circle and try to kick the ball back and forth to one another. This is a good game to play at family gatherings. Children are thrilled to play such "real" games with older kids and grown-ups.

*Approximate age range: 21 to 23 months*

# CLIMBING ON FURNITURE

Toddlers are programmed to climb on furniture. What they are doing is fulfilling their innate desire to exercise their gross motors skills in new and necessary ways. What they aren't doing is trying to wreck your furniture and drive you crazy, though these may seem like inevitable outcomes of their behavior.

So, instead of trying to prevent your child from climbing on furniture, you may as well give in to this impulse and let your child go full steam ahead. You can set limits and say that certain chairs and sofas may not be climbed on. Include in the list furniture that is too precious and too rickety.

Then stay back (but close) and let your child climb. If your child doesn't want to climb chairs, you might even gently encourage the activity by saying it's okay on certain chairs.

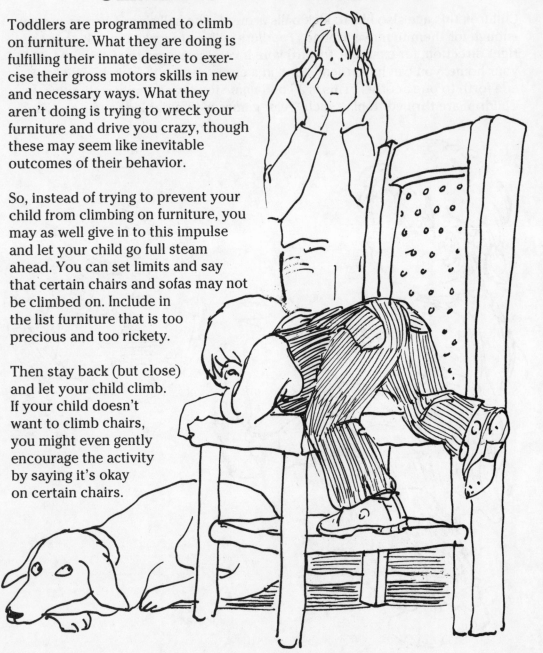

*Approximate age range: 21 to 23 months*

# HOW DO I GET DOWN?

Not being able to get down from a chair is a typical toddler problem. They can't handle what they get themselves into. And overreacting and saying, "Why did you climb up there in the first place?" is a typical parent problem. Todders can't get down because they haven't learned that skill—yet. But they will, and you can help by showing them how. Children this age can usually get down from a table or chair that is waist-high. Higher than that gets a little dicey.

*Approximate age range: 21 to 23 months*

# SORTING OBJECTS & SHAPES

Sorting objects is an intriguing activity for children at this stage. If you serve them a dish of peas and carrots, for example, you might see them carefully set the peas aside and eat only the carrots. If they have a collection of little cars, you might see them sort the cars into groups, perhaps by color, even before they actually know the names for colors. When you see a child performing sorting operations, you don't need to comment, but you might casually enrich the experience with comments such as: "The peas are green and round, and the carrots are orange and square."

But beware of interfering and ruining the experience for your child. If your child is absorbed in some sort of self-motivated and rather intellectual sorting activity, leave him or her alone. These kinds of activities are their own reward for children.

**Mailbox-type toys.**

Mailbox-type toys have holes in them of varying shapes that correspond to colorful little blocks of varying shapes. The child "posts" the shapes into the box through the correct holes. Observing your child play with such a toy will tell you if your child is able to perform the shape-matching task. If not, you can demonstrate it yourself and help your child, but don't push your child. In time, your child will be able to do it.

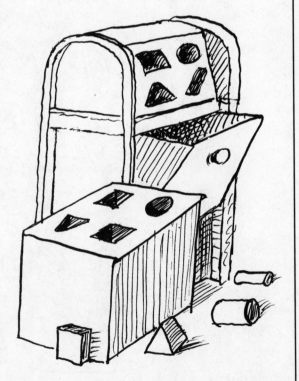

**Puzzles.**

Even the simplest puzzles may be too hard for your child to do alone at this age. Give help freely, and be patient. When your child is two, he or she will be more successful.

*Approximate age range: 21 to 23 months*

# SIMPLE SORTING GAMES

Sorting things is a common household task that your child can "help" you with, if you are willing. For example, children with clean hands can help you put the silverware away. Or they can help you put the lids to pots and pans away. Sorting toys in a messy room is a headache. With your child's help it can turn into a learning activity—if you're in the right mood and if you have the time. If you don't have the right mood and enough time, don't try it. You may prefer to sort silverware or pick up your child's room quietly all by yourself after your child goes to bed.

*Approximate age range: 21 to 23 months*

# COLORING WITH CRAYONS

Provide your child with fat crayons and paper to draw on. Observe what happens. When children first start to color, they usually make light strokes on paper. They grasp the crayon in their fist because they can't yet grasp it the way you do. Later, they'll be able to hold it in the more conventional way. Children are amazed by the simple lines they draw.

Anticipate problems in order to prevent them, and set limits from the start. When you give your child crayons, teach your child what is appropriate drawing behavior and what is not. Explain that crayons are for drawing on paper and not on walls or in books. If your child disobeys, take the crayons away until the child is willing to abide by your rules for coloring.

Sometimes paper slips around too much for children to draw upon it. You can solve this problem by using masking tape to hold the paper down. If you like, put on some music and draw with your child. Children often like to share a drawing with you. You make a few lines on paper, then your child makes a few more lines, and so on.

When your child is finished coloring, he or she should put the crayons away. Demonstrate this process enthusiastically, making the task seem like an interesting challenge. You may want to put the crayons away on a high shelf so that they can only be taken out by a grown-up.

*Approximate age range: 21 to 23 months*

# CHILDREN'S FIRST DRAWINGS

Your child's first drawings may not look so great to the rest of the world, but to you and your child, they are spectacular. Refrigerators make perfect galleries for children's art. Use nonstick masking tape or big magnets, and post the drawings where you and your child can peruse them. Talk about them together. You may soon have more drawings than your refrigerator can hold. Other uses? Wrapping paper, stationery for grandparents, framed pictures for presents for grandparents and friends.

*Approximate age range: 21 to 23 months*

# FRIENDS . . .

Young children like to play with other children, especially familiar children. They are fascinated by them. Sometimes all they do is stare at one another. Toddlers sometimes may not look like they are playing, but they are enjoying themselves. They also like to investigate one another's toys.

Sometimes the most successful pairings are of children of slightly different ages. The younger child enjoys observing the older one, and the older one enjoys being the more capable one.

*Approximate age range: 21 to 23 months*

# . . . AND ENEMIES

Young children can get mad, jealous, embarrassed, hurt, and just plain nasty. Sometimes they fight because their angry feelings overwhelm them. Sometimes they fight just for the experience of it. They've seen other kids hit each other, and they want to try that behavior themselves. And sometimes they fight because they are tired. The first thing to do when children fight is to separate them. Say, "No fighting," and offer an alternative: a snack, a different toy for each, a story, or possibly even a nap.

*Approximate age range: 21 to 23 months*

# FOOD PLAY—BAD

The enduring conundrum for parents of toddlers is how to set limits for those children who freely act out their ideas and emotions. Take mealtime. Feeding a toddler can go smoothly one day and be a nightmare the next. A child who knows how to eat now makes a complete mess of things, laughing and spitting and refusing to eat and even throwing food on the floor. What do you do when you are faced with a toddler who is losing it? Number one: Don't laugh. Number two: Take the food away, explaining simply that "food is not for playing; food is for eating." Don't overreact. Both yelling and spanking scare and hurt toddlers.

*Approximate age range: 21 to 23 months*

# FOOD PLAY—GOOD

Because children do like to touch food and prepare things with it, they enjoy "cooking" on their level. Toddlers can make these recipes, if you help them.

RAISINS and CHEESE CRACKERS

Goo. oo

* CRACKERS (or Toast)

* Raisins

* Cream Cheese

YOU spread a cracker with cream cheese, and your CHILD pokes raisins into the cheese.

YOGURT PUDDING

* Plain yogurt

* Jelly or Jam or Baby food or Canned fruit cocktail

YOU put some yogurt and jelly in a bowl. Your CHILD mixes it up.

BANANA CANDY

* Banana    * Yogurt    * Brown sugar (or chopped nuts, or wheat germ, or Toasted sesame seeds)

YOU slice the banana and place it in front of YOUR CHILD with a dish of yogurt and a dish of brown sugar. Your CHILD dips the banana slices first in the yogurt and then in the brown sugar.

*Approximate age range: 21 to 23 months*

# "WHAZZAT?"

At some point your toddler makes the brilliant discovery that absolutely everything has a name. And being a curious soul, your toddler now decides to learn all these names, or at least to ask about them. Not every name will be remembered, but your toddler loves to point at things and ask, "Whazzat?"

Answer, of course, briefly. You don't need to go into long explanations. A simple name will do. If you get the feeling, as you undoubtedly will at times, that your child is less interested in learning a name and more interested in getting you to respond, you might consider giving your child what he or she really needs, which probably is a little more attention. If your child is tormenting you with Whazzats, try distracting him or her with another activity.

*Approximate age range: 21 to 23 months*

# THE TODDLER INTERROGATOR

The same goes for the other favorite question that toddlers like to ask, "Why?" Does your child really want a full explanation of a particular phenomenon or parental directive, or is your child just saying a new and exciting word to get a response from you?

**Because I said so.**

"Because I said so" is a parent's last response to children demanding to know why they have to put on a hat, take a bath, or go to bed. After you have given the honest reason clearly several times (because it's cold, because you're dirty, because people need to sleep), you may find yourself saying what you hated to hear your parents say, "Because I said so." When you think about it, it's not a bad answer, but your child has you beat anyway by now saying, "Why?" In other words, why did you say so? Don't bother to explain. Give up, smile, hug your child, and start the water for the bath. In general, answer toddlers' questions about everyday events as simply as possible. Long-winded explanations go over their heads. Children will continue to ask why as they grow. When they are older, they will understand explanations better.

*Approximate age range: 21 to 23 months*

# SAYING SHORT SENTENCES

Many toddlers this age use three- or four-word sentences. They seem to grasp the idea of subject and verb. Exactly how this happens, no one knows; but all experts say that children need to hear language in order to learn how to use it. The more children hear, the more they begin to understand how language works. If you keep a tape recorder handy, you can record your child's words and sentences. If you record your child every month or so, you'll have a wonderful record of how your child learned to talk.

DOLLY GO BOOM

If you do make a tape of your child's developing language skills, consider sending a copy of it to grandparents and other relatives far away.

*Approximate age range: 21 to 23 months*

# LISTEN TO YOUR CHILD

Communication is a two-way street; it involves talking and listening. Don't tune out your child. Whether your child is an early talker, a late talker, or somewhere in the middle, pay attention and show that you care. If you want your child to listen to you, you have to listen to your child.

*Approximate age range: 21 to 23 months*

# MY VOCABULARY GROWS TO . . .

Your toddler may be able to say as many as twenty words now. The words may not be pronounced correctly, but they are real words that stand for people and things your child knows. Not all children say what they know out loud. A certain few seem to wait until they can speak well before they say a word. If you are worried about your child's progress, consult your pediatrician. Otherwise, enjoy your child's vocabulary, and, if you like, keep a pad handy to list the words your child is learning. In the coming months the list will grow longer and longer.

*Approximate age range: 21 to 23 months*

# . . . 20 WORDS

Make sure your child is immersed in a language-rich environment. You don't want your child to be bombarded with boring words all day long, but you do want your child to perceive the pleasures and intimacy of language. When you chat and play with your child, you provide exactly the right kind of language stimulation. TV, on the other hand, does not do the trick. It's too impersonal. Toddlers need you and other caring people to talk *with* them.

**Toddlers love chants.**

You can make up chants about anything. Just say the same sentence over and over with slight variations each time. Clap or bounce your child on your lap as you chant. Eventually your child will be able to chant with you.

*Approximate age range: 21 to 23 months*

# FEELINGS . . .

Learning how you feel about something is important to young children, who experience a full range of emotions before they are able to identify them. Learning that others, especially you, share the same kinds of comfortable and not-so-comfortable feelings is helpful. Your child copies you. If your child hears you talk about your feelings and watches you handle your feelings without hurting others, your child will learn that a variety of feelings are normal and that there are interesting words for describing them. Your child will learn that talking about feelings can help to alleviate them.

**Kicking, biting, hair pulling, and punching.**

Help your child understand that it's okay to feel angry, but that it's not okay to hurt others. Don't make the mistake of condoning harmful activities just because you understand your child's feelings. Hurtful behaviors are not allowed. Offer harmless alternatives, such as punching a pillow.

*Approximate age range: 21 to 23 months*

# . . . AND WORDS FOR THEM

WATCH OUT, MAX!

SOMETIMES I'M HAPPY!

SOMETIMES I COULD SCREAM!

I'M SO TIRED AND GRUMPY

SOMETIMES YOU MAKE ME SO MAD!

Don't forget to share your feelings of love and contentment as well as your feelings of frustration and anger. Sometimes fathers who love their children very much forget to convey their love to their children.

I'M SO GLAD I'M YOUR DADDY!

*Approximate age range: 21 to 23 months*

# HASSLES AND MESS

For some reason, some toddlers are fascinated with messes. They don't mind getting their hands all sticky and gooey. And they don't mind putting their sticky, gooey hands on the walls and on you. Because you often have to wipe their hands and faces, it's good to be prepared to do so, and not to be lacking a handkerchief or wipes just when you need them most.

**Be prepared.**

When you are out with your toddler for the afternoon, have what you need. You never know what's going to happen, and, as they say, it's better to be safe than sorry.

**What to pack for todder outings:**

Clothing
Diaper(s)
Wipes
Snack
Drink
Toy
Book

*Approximate age range: 21 to 23 months*

# A HASSLE-FREE GLUE PROJECT

Toddlers can do this gluing project quite neatly. Perhaps the reason they like it so much is that they get to use something sticky in a proper way.

**Materials needed:**

• White glue, such as Elmer's

• A little dish to put the glue in

• Paper plates, cardboard, or big junk-mail envelopes

• Little things, such as pine cones and little Styrofoam packing material peanuts. Start collecting these things now for future projects.

• Newspapers (optional)

**Directions:**

1. Tape newspaper to the table to protect the surface, if necessary.

2. Set out two paper plates (one for your child and one for you), a little dish with a little glue in it, and a pile of little things.

3. Demonstrate how to pick up a little thing, dip it gently in a little glue, and stick it to the paper plate. Your child will copy you and feel quite proud. The finished "sculpture" can be a present for someone. Your child may be happy to do your plate for you, if you stay close by.

*Approximate age range: 21 to 23 months*

# THE VALUE OF WATER PLAY

Water play is both fun and educational. When children play with water and water toys, they not only enjoy themselves, but they also learn about the physical qualities of water and concepts such as full and empty, floating and sinking, heavy and light, wet and dry. These concepts are strengthened in children if you provide interesting water toys and talk about them playfully.

Water play also vents feelings. Children can slap water, squish it, pour it quickly, and act out stories with it. Try putting your child with figure toys in the bath after watching TV cartoons. What the children have repressed may come out. Water play is also an excellent way to get clean.

Warning: Water play can be dangerous. Toddlers have drowned in inches of water. Supervise them closely. Also, watch that little toys don't go down the bathtub drain.

*Approximate age range: 21 to 23 months*

# Educational Water Play Toys

LITTLE PLASTIC BOTTLES THAT FIT THE HAND EASILY

CLEAR FLEXIBLE TUBING

EYE DROPPER

SPONGES

MEASURING CUP

PLASTIC FUNNEL

SQUEEZE BOTTLE

PLASTIC CUP AND SPOONS

PLASTIC CONTAINER WITH HOLES PUNCHED OUT

*Approximate age range: 21 to 23 months*

# WHAT KINDS OF TOYS . . .

*Approximate age range: 21 to 23 months*

# . . . ARE BEST FOR MY CHILD?

**A toddler toy checklist:**

The best toys for your child are those that meet the following criteria:

• They are developmentally appropriate for your child (see pages 30–31).

• They are too large to be swallowed.

• They have no *detachable* parts that can be swallowed.

• They have no little parts that can *break off* and be swallowed.

• They have no sharp edges or points.

• They are well made.

• They are not made of glass or brittle plastic.

• They are nontoxic.

• They have no parts that can pinch fingers or catch hair.

• They have no long cords that could accidentally strangle a young child.

If a toy does not meet the above criteria, it should be used by the child only under very close supervision.

**Toys for one-and-a-half-year-olds:**

Snap-lock beads & big wooden beads
Little figures & animals
Shape toys
Teddy bear
Big, simple dump truck
Small alphabet or number blocks
Push & pull toys

**Toys for two-year-olds:**

Safe riding toy
Cobbler's bench
House & barn for figures & animals
Paper & fat crayons
Doll
Small cars & trucks
Single shape puzzles

**Toys for two-and-a-half-year-olds:**

Big wooden blocks
Tea set
Punching toy
Easy puzzles
Small nonelectric toy train

**Toys for three-year-olds:**

Construction trucks
Toy wheelbarrow
Tricycle
Puppets
Toy tool bench
Simple lotto games

*Approximate age range: 21 to 23 months*

# INSTANT GAMES

Here are two games you can play with toddlers anywhere, anytime, no equipment needed, just a little space.

**Follow the leader.**

Have the kids make a parade with you as the leader. Ask them to do what you do and go where you go. As you parade around, say where you are going, as in, "Okay, here we go by the refrigerator, everyone touch the refrigerator, and now we're going under the table, everyone down on your hands and knees!"

**Ring around the rosie.**

Have the children stand in a circle and hold hands. Walk in a circle as you sing, "Ring around the rosie, Pockets full of posies, Ashes, ashes, All fall down!" The anticipation of and then the actual falling down is the best part for toddlers.

*Approximate age range: 21 to 23 months*

# INSTANT TOYS

Be on the alert for household objects that can be turned into instant toys. For example, an empty Band-Aid box with a little toy inside makes an instant shaker. Your child can change the contents to produce different sounds. Watch, though, that your child doesn't put little things in his or her mouth.

**Other toys that can be made from common household objects:**

• Cardboard toilet paper rolls can become telephones

• Cardboard paper towel rolls can become horns

• Milk cartons can be washed, dried, taped shut, and used for blocks

• Pot lids can become cymbals

• Small plastic detergent bottles with handles can be washed out and used for pouring water in the bathtub and toddler pool

• Old-fashioned, wooden peg clothespins can be little dolls, especially if you add facial features with a marker

*Approximate age range: 21 to 23 months*

# PUPPETS

WANNA
PLAY ?

Puppets provide an opportunity for dramatic play and affection. Big but light fuzzy puppets are like dolls and teddy bears; and the nice thing about them is that you can put your hand inside and make the puppet talk to your child. This is fascinating for children. Sometimes they want to try, too, to make the puppet talk to them and to you.

If you don't have a puppet, you can take an old white sock and draw a face on it with a marker. Don't worry if your artistic efforts are not earthshaking; they will be to your child because you have just made a sock come alive!

Children like stories about themselves, so if you're trying to think up a story for the puppet to tell, make your child the main character and include familiar people and happenings from your child's life.

*Approximate age range: 21 to 23 months*

# PETS

Pets provide children with a variety of learning experiences plus the joy of possession and, depending on the pet, relationship. However, your toddler won't be able to help much in the care of a pet until he or she is older. For now, children can learn from pets that pets are not toys and that animals have certain needs, such as food, sleep, cleanliness, and exercise. When pets give birth, they provide a natural course in sex education. If you want to get a pet, select one that will adapt to your family and home.

**Dogs.**

Certain dogs tolerate toddlers beautifully. Find out which ones these are by consulting pet store operators, veterinarians, and other pet owners.

**Cats.**

Cats that don't scratch and don't mind toddlers are the best. Get advice.

**Guppies, turtles, and tropical fish.**

Children like to watch them, but make sure your child can't reach in.

**Parakeets.**

With patience many of them can be taught to talk. Perhaps you and your child can do this together. The cage should be too high for your toddler to reach.

**Gerbils.**

Toddlers can watch but not touch yet. Make sure they can't get into the cage.

*Approximate age range: 21 to 23 months*

# MAKING BEAUTIFUL DESIGNS

This is potentially the messiest activity suggested in this book. It is also an activity that produces the most spectacular results. The project is easy to do; that's not the problem. The problem is that food coloring stains clothing—so if you attempt this, dress yourself and your child in stainable old clothes. Warning: It's also hard to wash food coloring off your hands. It comes off—but not right away.

1.

FOLD A PAPER NAPKIN ANY OLD WAY UNTIL IT IS A SMALL FOLDED OBJECT.

2.

DRIP FOOD COLORING ALONG THE EDGES, LETTING YOUR CHILD HOLD THE NAPKIN, WHILE YOU DRIP, OR VICE-VERSA. USE VARIOUS COLORS AND DRIP WHEREVER YOU WANT ON THE NAPKIN.

3. OPEN UP THE NAPKIN. THE COLORS WILL HAVE SOAKED THROUGH AND MADE A LOVELY DESIGN.

*Approximate age range: 21 to 23 months*

# MAKING SCRAPBOOKS TOGETHER & READING SCRAPBOOKS AS BOOKS

If you like to take pictures of your child, you might also like to make scrapbooks or photo albums. Instead of storing these albums away on a shelf for relatives and friends to see, why not take them down and "read" them to your toddler?

Include photos of your child's favorite people, pets, and objects. If you like, you can label the photos with words, but don't expect your toddler to read them. Still, it's okay for the words to be there for you to read . . . and for your child someday to read.

Sturdy albums with plastic-coated pages will best survive the use of a toddler. If you worry that your child will wreck the photos, have double prints made, and keep one set for posterity.

*Approximate age range: 21 to 23 months*

# TODDLERS LOVE BOOKS!

Bookstores and libraries have sections that feature books for toddlers. Many of the books are printed on nearly indestructible materials so that toddlers can handle them freely without inadvertently ripping them. It's nice for kids to have these books around and to have access to them, like toys.

PLASTIC, FOAM-FILLED "SOFT" BOOKS

CLOTH BOOKS

CARDBOARD BOOKS

*Approximate age range: 21 to 23 months*

# BOOKS & BEDTIME ROUTINES

Toddlers thrive on routine. They like to sense the pattern of their day so that they can feel secure within the structure and can anticipate what's coming next. Because children love books as well as routine, a pattern that works well for many children and their families is to have a bath, a story or two, and then good night. At bathtime you can discuss what books you'll read together.

*Approximate age range: 21 to 23 months*

# CHAPTER THREE:
# 24 TO 26 MONTHS

**Welcome to the terrible twos.**

No doubt, you have been warned about the terrible twos. Two-year-olds are legendary; they vie with adolescents as the most challenging age group to raise. Twos (and adolescents) are known for their tempestuous moods. You may have seen other toddlers have tantrums and sworn that your child never would. And, in fact, your child may pass through the next year without ever having one. If not, the advice offered in this chapter and others that follow will help you cope.

**Parents have temper tantrums, too.**

We all blow our cool sometimes. We try to be rational role models for our children, but there are days when our kids drive us nuts, and for a moment, we can't take it anymore. So, we shout, count to 100, frantically hand the child off to another adult, or put the child in a safe room and shut the door. We may feel momentarily like hurting our children, but we don't, because afterward, we're glad that we didn't because it's harmful, and useless, and because, when they're not being terrible, twos are absolutely terrific.

*Approximate age range: 24 to 26 months*

**Welcome to the terrific twos.**

The same little devil who drove you crazy an hour ago is now a little angel—calm, sweet, interested, friendly, loving, cooperative. Our children must learn from us that we can take them at their worst and that, while at times we don't approve of their behavior, we always love them.

Our children learn to take us at our worst, too, as long as our worst is not too bad. Tolerance and patience are outstanding qualities for children to learn. Our children need to trust that while we all flip out from time to time, we won't flip too far. We'll bounce back, and so will they.

*Approximate age range: 24 to 26 months*

# CELEBRATING A SECOND BIRTHDAY

**Hints for giving a succesful party:**

1. Keep it small and short. Two to four children for one hour is plenty. Tell parents specifically when the party begins *and ends*. Invite parents to stay.

2. Serve a simple snack, such as cupcakes with no frosting, ice cream cones (after the cupcakes), and juice. Put a tablecloth on the floor.

3. Play age-appropriate games, such as ring around the rosie and follow the leader (see page 80).

4. Take photographs or videos.

5. For favors, send guests home with large pretzels or paint-with-water books (see page 161).

*Approximate age range: 24 to 26 months*

# KEEP IT SIMPLE

Less is more. Less hype during the days and weeks before a party will bring more pleasant times during the party. Fewer people at the party will bring more contentment all around. Fewer presents, food, favors, and so on will bring to the party an element of peace. Less wound-up children, especially the birthday child, will bring more smiles.

*Approximate age range: 24 to 26 months*

# RIDING TOYS WITHOUT PEDALS

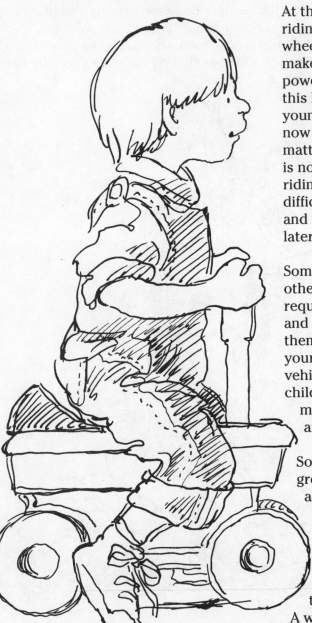

At this age the most desirable riding toys for children still have wheels but no pedals. Toddlers make the vehicles go with leg power. They may have been riding this kind of a toy since they were younger, or they may be riding it now for the first time. It doesn't matter. The most important thing is not to push your child into riding toys with pedals. They are difficult for toddlers to manage, and there is plenty of time for them later.

Some riding toys have four wheels, others have three. The basic requirement is that they are solid and that your toddler can manage them without tipping over. Watch your child as he or she tries the vehicles that belong to other children. See what seems to be the most comfortable, most fun, and safest for your child.

Some riding toys for this age group come with sirens and annoying horns. If your child rides at home and these sounds disturb the family too much (they can be loud!), you might want to dismantle them. After all, things do break sometimes. A white lie, but, hey, they're loud!

*Approximate age range: 24 to 26 months*

# WHAT TO DO WHEN YOUR CHILD CAN'T DO THINGS

When your child can't do things, you can usually psyche out the reason. Your child may be too tired to try, or too hungry, or too sick, or even too bored. Your child may have wanted to do something else. Or your child may find the task too hard. (See pages 30–31.) In any of these cases, the best thing to do is to stop the activity and move on to something else that suits your child's needs.

Sometimes, however, a child needs your help in doing something. If a puzzle, for example, is too hard, you can adapt it to fit your child's ability by helping him or her—in the same way that sometimes you might simpify a story when you realize it's going over your child's head. You can make a game of having your child hold your hand while you find the right place for the puzzle piece, and then together you can shout, "Wow!" The point is to make the experience successful for your child. In other words, make the experience doable.

*Approximate age range: 24 to 26 months*

# RUNNING AROUND

As children get older, they like to run around more and more. Often, it seems that they'd rather run than walk from one place to another. They need space to run around in so they like to be outside in the backyard or the park. They like to run around with other children, too. They seem to know that the best way to get stronger and better at running is to practice.

Given that your child has a safe space to run around in and some companions, you can rest on a park bench and supervise from there. Make sure they don't run out of your sight, though, which can happen quickly.

*Approximate age range: 24 to 26 months*

# WALKING BACKWARD

The first step forward is a well-celebrated happening in a child's life. But the first step backward, which usually happens in the coming months, often goes unnoticed. From time to time, show your child how to walk backward. Make it a fun activity, not a demanding one. Sooner or later, your child will be able to do it. Now you can play more games. Sit in a chair and say, "Can you walk backward to me?" This is fun for children because they don't know quite when they'll reach you. At that time, of course, you hug your child and maybe even engage in a little belly tickling, too. It's always good to supply language, such as: "You're getting closer, closer, closer . . . GOTCHA!"

*Approximate age range: 24 to 26 months*

# BOO-BOOS

Toddlers get little boo-boos—injuries that are not very serious. When they get them, the best thing to do is be calm. Don't overreact and scare your child. Acknowledge your child's feelings, and offer the best remedy there is for a boo-boo: a kiss. On a more serious level, you also should know how to treat cuts and bruises, have your doctor's number handy, and have thought through ahead of time where you would want to take your child in a medical emergency. It's wise to keep a first-aid book in your home.

*Approximate age range: 24 to 26 months*

# ATTITUDES ARE CATCHING

The way you see your child will be reflected in the way your child sees him- or herself. If there's something about the way your child looks that bothers you, discuss it with your wife, friend, and doctor, but don't discuss it in front of your child. Your child hears things you may not realize she is hearing. Be positive about your child to your child.

*Approximate age range: 24 to 26 months*

# VERY SIMPLE PUZZLES

**Single-shape puzzles.**

These puzzles have big pieces that each depict one object, such as an apple or a bear. Sometimes each piece has a tiny knob on top. The handles make it easier for young children to manipulate the pieces.

**Puzzles you can make.**

Cut an old calendar picture into four pieces. Show your child the picture with the pieces put together. Then mix up the pieces and help your child put them back in order. Make sure the picture is comprehensible to your child.

*Approximate age range: 24 to 26 months*

# LOTTO

Lotto is a simple game, easy enough for toddlers to play. To play lotto, children match pictures with pictures. To make the most of the game, you can play too, helping your child match and name the objects as they are matched. Lotto games are usually found near the puzzles in toy stores.

It's also easy to make lotto games. All you need are sets of matching pictures. Paste one set on a cardboard base, and use the other set as matching cards. You can make the cards more sturdy by pasting them on index cards and cutting them out. The next time you receive two copies of the same catalog, don't throw one away. Use the catalogs to make lotto games.

A more complicated kind of lotto is where you match pictures to letters, or numerals to sets of objects that contain the right amount. These games are for future years. For now, matching pictures is enough.

*Approximate age range: 24 to 26 months*

# OLD-FASHIONED PEGBOARDS ARE FUN FOR CHILDREN THIS AGE

You and your parents both may remember playing with pegs and pegboards in your childhoods. This toy continues to fascinate children today. They have the manual dexterity to pick up the pegs and insert them into the little holes on the pegboard. They may like to fill up the entire pegboard or to make simple designs with different color pegs. There are more modern variations of this game, usually involving somewhat bigger plastic pegs. These are fun, too.

*Approximate age range: 24 to 26 months*

# SO ARE BIG WOODEN BEADS

Both pegboards and big wooden beads help children strengthen eye-hand coordination. Threading a lace through a bead involves some of the same skills required for inserting a peg in a pegboard. The beads should be about one inch in diameter with large holes for easy stringing. If the laces are difficult to thread, your child will need, and enjoy, your help. The beads don't have to be wooden; plastic ones are fine, too. As your child grows, he or she can make necklaces with patterns and also can try to match a pattern that you draw or make yourself. But for now, just make simple necklaces together.

*Approximate age range: 24 to 26 months*

# CARPENTRY & CHILDREN

You can buy or make little toy carpentry benches for children. The best ones have pegs that can be hammered into holes with a wooden mallet, big screws that can be screwed by hand easily into big threaded holes, and a pegboard with pegs. Commercial carpentry benches for children this age are quite safe. If you make a carpentry bench for your child, follow directions for one made for toddlers. Be sure all parts are safe and easy for your child to work.

When your child is about five or six, you can build small wooden toys and birdhouses together. Children like to learn how to use real tools, but they need you right there with them every moment because real tools can be dangerous.

*Approximate age range: 24 to 26 months*

# TAPE COLLAGE

Masking tape is a great, inexpensive collage material for toddlers. They can rip off pieces and stick them down all by themselves. They can lift off pieces of their designs and rearrange them. Do not squander this useful resource. Save it for when you're on the phone with a client or the plumber and when you need your child to be quiet. In fact, it's not a bad idea to keep a roll of masking tape in your office or near the phone. You might even want to have different colors of it. If your child can't rip the tape, you can probably do it and talk on the phone at the same time, right?

*Approximate age range: 24 to 26 months*

# PLAYING WITH DOLLS

Dolls enable children to enjoy feeling grown-up and nurturing—like you! Most people today recognize that boys as well as girls relate to dolls. If you like, you can provide your toddler with anatomically correct boy dolls.

**Doll clothes.**

It's not easy for toddlers to take clothes off of dolls if the clothing is too complicated or too tight. You might want to suggest that your child put some of his or her own clothes on the doll, perhaps old clothes that are outgrown.

**Clothing toys.**

Some dolls are made with special clothes that are designed to help children practice the skills of manipulating buttons, zippers, laces, socks, and shoes. Certain baby books help children learn these skills, too.

*Approximate age range: 24 to 26 months*

# DRESS-UP

Children like to play dress-up, trying on different clothes that belong to special people, such as parents, grandparents, clowns, firefighters, police officers, dancers, and so on. Start a collection of dress-up clothes in a big box or basket. Add to it over the years. Dress-up is a good dramatic play activity for toddlers to enjoy with their friends. So, for now, only put dress-up clothes into the basket that they can handle, or else be prepared to help them.

Simple dress-up items for toddlers are hats, scarves, and mittens. Children particularly like hats that represent different jobs, such as firefighter hats and cowboy hats.

*Approximate age range: 24 to 26 months*

# *I Can Take Off My Shoes . . .*

As irritating as toddlers can be, you have to feel sorry for them. They inadvertently set themselves up for failure. No wonder they sometimes get so mad! In their desire to learn new things and experience the world, they get into situations that they can't control. In this way they frustrate both themselves and their parents.

You often see this problem acted out by toddlers in the realm of dressing and undressing. Clothes are physical, and some toddlers are very aware of certain textures touching their skin. Often, if they don't want to be wearing a particular item of clothing, they will just take it off. Other times they'll take off clothing just for the heck of it. And sometimes they'll take it off merely because they can—or think they can and want to try.

Once they get their shoes or clothes off, they may not be able to put them back on again. Sometimes they don't care, but you do. And sometimes you don't care, but they do, which you, no doubt, will hear about.

*Approximate age range: 24 to 26 months*

# ... *But I Can't Put Them Back On*

When you are in a hurry to go somewhere and your child has just taken off his or her shoes, you may feel your blood pressure start to rise. "I just put those shoes on you!" you shout. "Why did you take them off?" Your toddler starts to cry, and you feel like crying, too. These are the little times that try a parent's soul.

One thing you can do is acknowledge your child's predicament. Saying it aloud may help your child understand the situation. You might say something like, "You have learned to take off your shoes, and that's good. But now is not the time to do that. Tonight when you go to bed, you can take off your shoes all by yourself. Now, I'm going to put them back on, and I'd like you to leave them on, okay?"

If your toddler won't cooperate and it's time to leave, stick the shoes in your pocket and carry your toddler. You can't win 'em all.

*Approximate age range: 24 to 26 months*

# IMITATING WHAT ADULTS DO

Children want to grow up. They want to become big people and do what big people do. Consequently, they like to have child-size tools and work equipment. They like little brooms and rakes that work. They like little gardening tools, tea sets, pots and pans, and furniture that looks like adult furniture.

They also like to go to adult places, such as stores and offices, with you. But if you take your child with you to your office, don't expect that he or she will play quietly in a corner while you work. Toddlers can't do that, so just stop by for a short visit.

*Approximate age range: 24 to 26 months*

# HOW TO DRIVE A CAR

Get a big box. Climb in. Hold on to a hoop or toy driving wheel, and drive!
Large empty boxes provide good opportunities for children to act out fantasies. Boxes can be cars one minute, trains the next, and then a house—all in
short order. All you need to do is provide the box and make a suggestion.

*Approximate age range: 24 to 26 months*

# WATCH YOUR LANGUAGE . . .

Your attitude toward your wife and women in general is the model your child sees and hears. Different families have different arrangements for sharing household work. Whatever your arrangement is, your child is learning from it. If you refuse to help out at home, you can be sure that your child sees that. If you are critical of your wife's efforts, you can be sure that your child sees that, too. By your behavior, you teach your child what men and fathers are like.

*Approximate age range: 24 to 26 months*

# . . . AND YOUR ACTIONS

There's nothing wrong with a little healthy anger freely expressed. But again, be aware that your child may be watching you. Anger that gets out of control is frightening to a child. Sometimes knowing that your child is watching you can be the factor that helps you decide to stay cool and maintain control. In this way, children can inspire us as parents to get our acts together.

*Approximate age range: 24 to 26 months*

# FOLLOWING SIMPLE COMMANDS

Two-year-olds are now able to follow simple commands, such as "Give me the crayon" and "Put the spoon in the bowl." They comprehend what you want, and often they oblige obediently. Reward such positive behavior with praise. The praise doesn't have to be lavish; it can just be an appreciative smile and a simple "Thanks." Sometimes your toddler will not oblige you. Before you get angry, check to make sure that your child has heard you, understands what you want, and that your request is reasonable. If your child still won't do what you want, offer a distraction, such as a toy in exchange for the remote, or get what you want by yourself, ignoring your child's truculence.

*Approximate age range: 24 to 26 months*

# PLEASE & THANK YOU

*Please* and *thank you* are often presented to children as magic words, and in a way, they are. They make people feel good. When your child takes a gift from you, you can ask, "What do you say?" Teach your child to say, "Thank you," or just "Thanks." He or she may not be able to pronounce it correctly and may not even understand what it means, but your child will grasp the notion of when it is appropriate to say it and that the word makes you happy. The same goes for "Please" when your child wants something. And, of course, it goes without saying, if you want your child to use the words *please* and *thank you*, you have to use them yourself.

*Approximate age range: 24 to 26 months*

# USING THE THIRD PERSON

Two-year-olds do not understand when to use the personal pronoun "I" to say, for example, "I go out." They refer to themselves in the third person and will do so probably until they are about three and a half. Their sentences now usually contain two to four words.

MARIA GO OUT!

*Approximate age range: 24 to 26 months*

# EXPERIENCE & LANGUAGE

Young children learn from concrete experiences. They can learn what *doggie* means by looking at a picture, but the learning is deeper and more meaningful if they learn the word from real-life experience. Everywhere you go with your child is an opportunity for you to introduce your child to new words: *gas pump, corn flakes, tomato, monkey, shell, shovel, pizza, tortilla.*

*Approximate age range: 24 to 26 months*

# LIBRARIES & BOOKSTORES

Two of the best places to take your toddler are the bookstore and the library. Many of these places have special read-aloud times for toddlers. Such events provide an opportunity for you to meet other parents and for your child to meet other toddlers, as well as for both of you to enjoy books.

*Approximate age range: 24 to 26 months*

# TAPES & VIDEOS

There are many high-quality records, cassette tapes, and CDs for young children. Libraries may have copies that you can borrow.

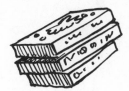

**Musical recordings.**

Listening to children's musical recordings with your child can help you learn the words and tunes to sing together at other times. Get recommendations from preschool teachers who know which tapes and CDs are good. Look for recordings made by the following artists and shows:

Hap Palmer
Raffi
Ella Jenkins
Greg & Steve
Shari Lewis
Rosenshontz
Sharon, Lois, and Bram
*Sesame Street*
*Barney*

**Videos.**

Look for videos made by the artists and groups named above. They can be trusted to produce quality programs. Call Kidvidz (800-914-5678) to obtain a semiannual four-page guide on more videos recommended by experts.

**Stories.**

Look for book and tape combinations. The advantage of these is that children can enjoy having the book read to them by you, and you can both listen to it in the car while you're driving.

*Approximate age range: 24 to 26 months*

# QUALITY TIME?

Quality time is when you and your child both do the same thing and you give your child your full attention. Now, no parent can provide quality time all the time. That would be too hard on both the parent and the child, who would end up craving a few minutes behind the couch with her doll while Dad watched TV. But all children need some quality time each day. Your child will let you know if he or she isn't getting enough by whining, clinging, and using other toddler tactics to demand your attention.

*Approximate age range: 24 to 26 months*

# CHORES CAN BE FUN

Doing chores with your toddler can be fun—on three conditions: 1) that you have enough time, 2) that there's something your toddler can really do, and 3) that the chore doesn't last too long. If you're trying to get a job done fast, you will only be annoyed at your toddler's ineptness. Toddlers don't just stand and wait. If there's nothing for them to do, they will find something to do, and it probably will be something that drives you crazy.

*Approximate age range: 24 to 26 months*

# CHEFS FOR THE DAY

Children love to cook because they get to experience new things to touch, smell, and taste. They also get to experience how ingredients change when they're mixed and baked. So cooking is great for children, but remember, when you bake with children, everything takes three times longer.

*Approximate age range: 24 to 26 months*

# WHERE DOES FOOD COME FROM?

Kids today can enter first grade without knowing where food comes from. They think orange juice and peas come from boxes in the refrigerator. Help your child make the connection between food and nature at an early age.

*Approximate age range: 24 to 26 months*

# GOOD DAYS

Good days are when your child plays with other children at your house, and no one fights and it doesn't rain . . .

and no one gets hurt, and no one clings to you . . .

and no one refuses to eat the crackers you offer, and no one spills a cup over . . .

and no one throws up, and all the parents come on time to pick up their kids.

*Approximate age range: 24 to 26 months*

# BAD DAYS

Bad days are when you wanted to work quietly at home, but the day care closed because of freezing rain, and two parents asked if you could watch their kids too, and you couldn't go out, and your daughter wouldn't share her new doll, not even for a minute, and one boy cried all day for his mommy, and the other boy was a biter, and because of the weather your wife and the other two parents all came home two hours later than anticipated. The truth is, all parents have good days and, unfortunately, all parents have bad ones, too.

*Approximate age range: 24 to 26 months*

# CHAPTER FOUR:
# 27 TO 29 MONTHS

Watching toddlers play with water and sand at the edge of a stream or at the beach is to understand how young children learn. They are like little professors, engaged in research. They don't need you to tell them about gravity; they will experience it as they pour sand from a shovel into a pail. Watching fathers at the water's edge is to understand their many roles, too.

**Dad as research assistant.**

As your child's research assistant, you hand your child tools that you know will work. You might suggest a variation of an activity. If you see the sand drying out, you might wet it with a little water. You don't direct the activity; you supplement it.

**Dad as tour guide.**

There are other roles you can play at the water's edge. First of all, your child didn't get there alone. You picked the spot and provided the transportation. You will watch out for the safety of your charge and get him or her home safely when the time is right. You have provided for food and snacks and, yes, like any good tour guide, you have thought about toileting considerations.

**Dad as talk show host.**

Did you ever notice how talk show hosts sit forward when they listen to their guests and how they maintain eye contact? They do this for a reason: It works. Both grown-ups and children respond when they feel their words are being listened to eagerly. Try it. Listen to your child talk about water and sand and mud as if he or she were the star of a talk show. You may want to do this for a while on site, and also later when you're home and reviewing the day.

**Dad as media hound.**

Well, why not? Indulge yourself. Take photos. Take videos. Write a journal. It's fun, and your productions will be enjoyed for years and years.

*Approximate age range: 27 to 29 months*

*Approximate age range: 27 to 29 months*

# JUMP!

Around this age many children begin to learn to jump. They experiment by lifting both feet off the ground and jumping in place. This is an exciting accomplishment for them and one you might miss if you weren't alerted to it. When toddlers first discover that they can (more or less) jump, they are quite amusing to watch. This is a good time to get out the video camera. You might want to record other current physical accomplishments, too: walking forward, walking backward, and running.

*Approximate age range: 27 to 29 months*

126

# 2 JUMPING (POPPING) SONGS

Children like to act out songs in physical ways. These two songs offer practice in jumping. Toddlers like to anticipate the moment in the song when they are supposed to jump.

**"Pop Goes the Weasel."**

All around the cobbler's bench; the monkey chased the weasel.
The monkey thought 'twas all in fun; POP! *(jump)* goes the weasel.

A penny for a spool of thread; a penny for a needle.
That's the way the money goes; POP! *(jump)* goes the weasel.

**"Popcorn Song."**
*(sung to the tune of*
*"I'm a Little Teapot")*

I'm a little popcorn in a pot.
Heat me up and watch me pop.
When I get all fat and white, I'm done.
Popping corn is lots of fun.
POP! *(jump)*
POP! POP! POP!
*(keep jumping)*

*Approximate age range: 27 to 29 months*

# TURNING DOORKNOBS

Toddlers get better and better at eye-hand coordination. Their manual dexterity improves to the point where they can unscrew little jar lids that aren't fastened too tightly and turn doorknobs. This is the time to make extra sure that any jars you don't want your child to open are put safely out of reach and any doors you don't want your child to open are locked.

*Approximate age range: 27 to 29 months*

# BEDROOM PRIVACY

There may be certain times when
you'd rather not have your child
enter your bedroom. For that reason,
now is the time to install a latch on
*your* side of the door. A latch gives
you a little time to get ready
for . . .

 . . . a visiting toddler.

*Approximate age range: 27 to 29 months*

# IMITATING OTHER CHILDREN

Toddlers are watchers and doers. They frequently try to copy what they see because imitation is one of the main ways they learn. Unfortunately, you can't always control what they see.

Sooner or later, your child will see and try to imitate activities that you may not approve of. Older children acting out pretend violence provide some of the most vivid scenes a toddler can watch. If you feel strongly, for example, that fantasy gun play is too "old" for your child to witness, you can take your child to the toddler section of the park instead and generally avoid places where older children play. As your child grows, you will have plenty of opportunity to talk with your child about what he or she sees in the world about you. You will have time to discuss the meanings of things and what your feelings are about right and wrong.

*Approximate age range: 27 to 29 months*

# TOILETING

Watching how older children take care of themselves can help toddlers learn what they need to learn in order to grow. Give your child a chance to copy the positive behaviors of older children. Sometimes a sympathetic older sibling can help immeasurably in the toilet training of a toddler. At this age many toddlers are able to let you know when they need to go to the toilet.

An interesting new (1993) picture book for chidren on the subject of toilet training is *Everyone Poops* by Taro Gomi. Check it out in the bookstore or library; it's not for everyone, but toddlers, who are not squeamish, are fascinated.

*Approximate age range: 27 to 29 months*

# PLAYMATES

We all want our children to be liked by others and to have friends. One of the most intriguing aspects of being a parent is watching your child in relationships with peers. Some children make friends easily; others are shy and take more time. Some children only want to play with familiar children; others will play with anyone. Some children like to be with other children most of the time; others are content to play alone. To find out how your child is with others, carefully observe him or her. When you do this, try to stay in the background and try to be nonjudgmental. See your child as a separate person, not a clone of yourself. Just because you were gregarious in your youth doesn't mean your child will be the same way.

If you see that your child seems to want to play with others but has trouble doing so, you can help in subtle ways. One thing you can do is start playing with something you know your child likes. Children this age, for example, like to pour water from little plastic teapots into little plastic cups. If another child wants to join in the fun, you can let that child take your place, thereby uniting the two children in play. Stay close by as long as your child needs you there.

*Approximate age range: 27 to 29 months*

# PLAY DATES

If you want your child to be invited to play at other children's homes, you have to be prepared to invite one or two other children to your home. It takes a little practice to supervise a play date successfully. Here's some advice to help you get started.

- **Safety comes first.**

Whatever you do with the children, be sure that it's safe. Keep your eye on the children at all times.

- **Set out a variety of toys that toddlers like.**

Children this age often play together in the same space but with separate toys. When they tire of a toy, they move on to something else. Be prepared to suggest alternative toys to children who want what another child is already using.

- **Have simple snacks available that are easy to serve.**

Raisins, hard crackers, bananas, and apple juice in cups are good. Ask parents to bring bottles if their children still use them.

- **Keep play dates short.**

One or two hours is enough at first.

*Approximate age range: 27 to 29 months*

# DRAWING WITH CRAYONS

At this age many children will scribble and draw circles with a crayon. A fat crayon is still best. If you draw a line on a piece of paper and ask your child to draw one like it, chances are your child will be able to comply. If your child likes this kind of copying activity, you can make a cross and other very simple designs to copy. This is more of a prewriting kind of activity than it is an artistic activity. To encourage artistic freedom, just let your child draw however he or she wants. All you need to provide are crayons of different colors and lots of paper.

CAN YOU DO THIS? FIRST ONE LINE AND THEN ANOTHER ACROSS IT...

*Approximate age range: 27 to 29 months*

# REACTING TO EARLY ART

You can, of course, rave about your child's early artistic creations, but another way to respond is to show your respect by commenting on the pictures. "Hm-m-m," you might say. "Look at that blue line. What a fine blue line it is. And here's an orange line, and look, there's a little red squiggle." By talking about your child's art work, you demonstrate your interest and supply descriptive language, as well.

*Approximate age range: 27 to 29 months*

# Clay, Play-Doh & Play Dough

### Real clay.

Not only is most potter's clay too hard and messy for toddlers to play with, but it also dries out. If you want to buy real clay, make sure it is nonhardening.

### Play-Doh.

Play-Doh is a modeling material that is less messy than clay. It comes in bright colors and smells weird. Kids like Play-Doh. Competitive products may be labeled just Dough. Store Dough and Play-Doh in the containers they come in, and make putting all the bits and pieces of Play-Doh back into the containers the last part of any Play-Doh activity.

### Play dough.

You can make play dough yourself (see opposite page). It's cheap and works just fine.

Clay, Play-Doh, and play dough are great art materials for toddlers. Kids can push, pull, smash, and form objects with them readily. They like to make snakes, worms, hot dogs, hamburgers, pancakes, peas, faces, balls, snowmen, and monsters. Provide toothpicks to stick in the monsters, but supervise the use of toothpicks carefully.

*Approximate age range: 27 to 29 months*

# How to Make Play Dough

Many fathers think they would never make play dough. But when you're stuck with a few toddlers on a rainy day and you can't think of anything interesting to do, making play dough can be fun. All that is required are inexpensive household ingredients that you probably already have on hand. Teach toddlers not to eat play dough, unless you make peanut butter play dough, which can be eaten.

**Play dough recipe:**

Mix 1/2 cup water with 1 tablespoon salad oil. Stir in 2 cups flour and 3/4 cup salt. Work with your hands until the mixture is smooth and thick as bread dough. If necessary, add more water. Have children wash their hands before they mix and play with the dough. Store the dough in a plastic bag in the refrigerator. If children have colds, throw the dough out.

**Peanut butter play dough recipe:**

Mix 1 cup honey, 2 cups instant nonfat dry milk, and 2 cups peanut butter in a bowl. Have the children (with clean hands) make little cookie shapes. Arrange them on a dish, refrigerate until supper, and serve for dessert.

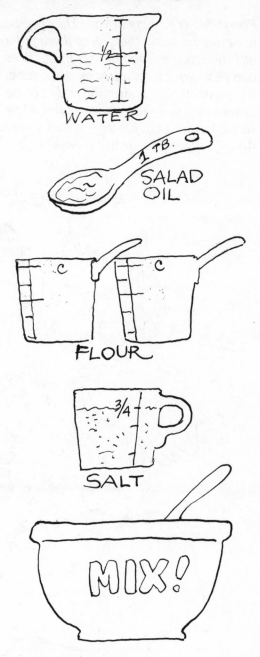

*Approximate age range: 27 to 29 months*

# FUSSY EATERS

*Everybody is looking at you. They are begging you to eat. But you don't eat. You are more powerful than all of them put together. You can get them all to pay attention to you—and only you!* Children are not stupid. One of the ways they can push your buttons is by not eating. Before you let this happen, consider the possibilities: your child may not be hungry or may not like the food. In the latter case, you may want to offer a few alternatives, but don't go overboard. As for the first case, forget it. Let your child get down from the high chair and don't play into his or her power trip.

*Approximate age range: 27 to 29 months*

# EATING IN THE CAR

Before you leave on trips, prepare a bag of snacks to assuage hunger attacks in the car. Choose snacks, like those suggested below, that your toddler can eat in his or her car seat without making too much of a mess.

I'M HUNGRY!

HARD, NON-CRUMBLY COOKIES and CRACKERS.

Soft cookies crumble and spill and make an awful mess.

•BANANAS•
Only if your child will eat them by him or herself, and not be tempted to squish them all over the car...

JUICE
IN A NON-SPILL CUP OR BOTTLE

Even if your child is off the bottle, he or she can enjoy it in the car, and you won't have to worry about spilling.

*Approximate age range: 27 to 29 months*

# LISTENING TO SOUNDS

When you're out and about in the world with your toddler, discuss not only the wonderful things you see together, but also the wonderful noises and sounds you hear. Toddlers like to hear you imitate the sounds of trains, cars, airplanes, trucks, horns, church bells, and, most of all, animals. Children love to learn the sounds of different animals—primarily through real-life experience but also through pictures in books. With books, you have to provide the sound for each animal. Soon you'll be able to ask your child, "What does the cow say?"

*Approximate age range: 27 to 29 months*

# LISTENING GAMES

Invent listening games for your child. The basic idea behind each game is for your child to identify an object out of sight by its sound.

**Close your eyes.**

Have your child put his or her hands over his or her eyes. Then have someone in the family say something like "teddy bear." Ask your child, "Who said that?"

**Hidden objects.**

Put a sound maker in a bag or behind your back. Ask your child, "What do you hear that I'm hiding behind my back?" Good items to hide: an alarm clock, a rattle, a stuffed animal that squeaks, a little bell, a tambourine. For the game to work, your child has to know about these things ahead of time.

*Approximate age range: 27 to 29 months*

# MY VOCABULARY GROWS TO 300 WORDS

Watch for the emergence of more sophisticated understandings and word usages.

**New words.**

Most of the words your toddler learns are the names of familiar objects: sock, shoe, fork, button, hat. Your child may understand but not be able to say all these new words.

**Prepositions.**

If you say, "The ball is under the couch," does your child understand what the word *under* means? Play games to help your child comprehend words that tell where things are. Hide a ball in different, easy places and use various prepositions, such as *on top of* and *behind,* to help your child find it.

*Approximate age range: 27 to 29 months*

# HOLIDAYS & LANGUAGE ENRICHMENT

Holidays provide exciting changes in daily routines. Children enjoy them most when the new and different events are not overstimulating and when holiday preparations are simple enough for children to share and enjoy. The simpler things are, the richer they are for children because there's time for them to absorb and learn words that go with the new experiences.

PS: While the toddler above is in full costume, many toddlers do not like all-encompassing costumes and face masks. So, when you think costumes, it's best to start simple and see how your child feels, literally.

*Approximate age range: 27 to 29 months*

# SHARING YOUR LIFE

Sharing means sharing, not imposing. It won't work to impose your favorite activity on your toddler. But if you have patience and understand your child's needs, you may be able to enjoy your favorite pastimes together. For example, if you want to watch a game on TV while taking care of your child, make sure your child has safe, interesting toys close by as well as food for snacks. When your child needs attention, be prepared to supply it. Cuddle your child on your lap, and teach your child how to cheer. But don't expect your child to understand the game, and be prepared ahead of time for inevitable interruptions. During critical moments, your child *will* need a diaper change. That's life. That's fatherhood. That's the ball game. Don't fight it. If you can't be flexible, don't watch your kid and a ball game at the same time.

PS: If your team loses, don't go ballistic. See yourself through your child's wondrous eyes. Do you like what you see?

*Approximate age range: 27 to 29 months*

# PLAYING CARDS WITH TODDLERS

You may have in mind a card game, such as slapjack to teach your child. But in fact your toddler is probably too young for that game. Your child likes to put cards in cardboard boxes and take them out again. Your child likes to pretend he or she knows what numbers are on cards. Observe what your child likes to do with cards, and see if you can play that game, too.

**3 toddler card games:**

**Post office.**

You prepare the "post office" by cutting a slot in a cardboard box. You and your child then "mail" the cards by putting them in the slot.

**Red cards and black cards.**

Match them.
That's all.

THREE!

**Numbers.**

Pick up a
card
and say its
number.
Your child
can't do this
but likes to
anyway!

*Approximate age range: 27 to 29 months*

# TALKING ABOUT PROCESS

When in doubt about what to discuss with your child, talk about what you are doing. Talking about the process of things gives children a sense of sequence and the connection between the steps of a process. Sometimes talking out loud about what you're going to do helps you organize yourself, too.

*Approximate age range: 27 to 29 months*

# REPEAT AFTER ME

Use repetitive chants to help your child develop descriptive language skills *and* (and this is important) to become more cooperative. In this chant, you say something from your child's point of view and then your child repeats it.

You: *A scarf to keep my neck warm.*
Child: *A scarf to keep my neck warm.*
You: *A hat to keep my head warm.*
Child: *A hat to keep my head warm.*
You: *Buttons to keep my coat together.*
Child: *Buttons to keep my coat together.*
You: *Mittens to keep my hands warm.*
Child: *Mittens to keep my hands warm.*
You: *Boots to keep my toes warm.*
Child: *Boots to keep my toes warm.*

Adapt the chant for getting undressed, such as:

You: *Off comes the scarf that kept me warm.*
Child: *Off comes the scarf that kept me warm.*

Your child will not speak as clearly or as well as you do, but don't be critical. Accept your child's language as is. Chanting should be fun!

*Approximate age range: 27 to 29 months*

147

# LOOKING AT THINGS UP CLOSE

Toddlers see the world up close, and they like to touch it. When you take a toddler to the park or out in the backyard, be prepared to sit down and look at individual things, such as acorns, leaves, stones, sticks, and seashells. Also be on the alert to be sure that your toddler doesn't try to eat these things.

Don't hurry. If you feel impatient, disappointed that instead of having a nice, brisk outdoor walk, here you are sitting, take a deep breath and relax. This time outdoors is for your toddler, who needs to stop and study things.

*Approximate age range: 27 to 29 months*

# TALKING ABOUT NATURE

The more you talk to your child about nature, the more your child will learn about it—and the more complex this learning will be.

## The names of things.

By hearing you name things casually, your child will learn that different things in nature have different names and will eventually be able to say these names.

## The variety of things.

By hearing you talk about the colors and shapes of things, your child will begin to learn descriptive words and to appreciate variety in nature.

## The organization of things.

By watching you sort objects, for example, putting shells with shells and stones with stones, your child will begin to learn to sort and classify objects.

## The connection between things.

By listening to you talk about seeds and plants, your child will begin to learn about the life cycle. Of course, this learning will be only on a toddler level, but that level forms the basis for more learning to come.

## Grow plants together.

Let your toddler use a toy rake to imitate you at work in the garden. If you don't have a garden, grow some plants on the windowsill, and let your child help you water them, using a little pitcher.

## From garden to the table.

Every now and then, pick peas, strawberries, corn, or other food plants, and prepare them for supper. Show the connection between the earth and what we eat.

SHELLING PEAS

TWO PEAS

ONE PEA

*Approximate age range: 27 to 29 months*

# CHILDREN NEED CLUES

Children need to know what's happening because they want to make sense of the world. They can't see patterns where there are none. They need to keep basically the same schedule every day, and they need your behavior to be fairly predictable. They like you to tell them what's going to happen next, and they like to be able to trust your words. Changes, of course, are inevitable. Holidays change life. Baby-sitters come and go. People move. Parents take trips. Such changes cannot be helped, but what helps children cope with these changes is the constancy of what they *usually* experience.

JIMMY, WHEN YOU WAKE UP, WE'LL GO FOR A RIDE IN THE TRUCK..

*Approximate age range: 27 to 29 months*

# FAMILY MEALS

Modern families often have trouble establishing daily routines. Fathers and mothers may work late. Parents' jobs may be at different times, and jobs may change. Relatives living with the family may come and go. With all the hustle and bustle of daily existence, families may not get a chance to sit down with one another and share even one meal a week. If your family has this problem, try to figure out a solution because children need consistent family rituals and routines. Think of family meals as a gift that you need to give your child at least three or four times every week.

*Approximate age range: 27 to 29 months*

# THE 3 MAJOR HURDLES: EATING . . .

In an ideal world, parents would soar with their toddlers over all hurdles. The toddlers would eat everything put before them, sleep through the night, and become toilet trained within a week. However, it's not an ideal world; and most parents and toddlers soar over only two of the three hurdles; some soar over only one. The one or two major hurdles left are stumbled over.

*Approximate age range: 27 to 29 months*

# . . . SLEEPING, AND TOILET TRAINING

Fortunately, however, by the time toddlers metaphorphosize into high school graduates, no one remembers or cares which hurdles they soared over and which hurdles they missed. If, currently, you are stressed out by one, two, or three of the three normal problems, be reassured. Eventually your child will eat vegetables, sleep well, and go to the toilet at night without waking you up.

*Approximate age range: 27 to 29 months*

# A Big Toy Box vs . . .

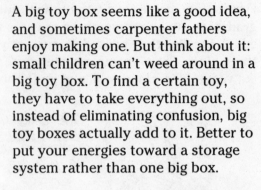

WHY DON'T YOU PUT ALL THE PEOPLE BACK IN THE CASTLE AND I'LL PUT AWAY YOUR ANIMALS..

A big toy box seems like a good idea, and sometimes carpenter fathers enjoy making one. But think about it: small children can't weed around in a big toy box. To find a certain toy, they have to take everything out, so instead of eliminating confusion, big toy boxes actually add to it. Better to put your energies toward a storage system rather than one big box.

A toy storage system enables you at the end of a hectic afternoon to sort toys and store them away for future use. That way, at the next play time, you can bring out only a few toys and sets of toys. When your child's interest in the toys diminishes, you can put away those toys and bring out new ones. Newly introduced sets of toys are more interesting to children than a mixture of toys scattered across the floor of a room.

When storing toys, keep similar toys together: little cars in a shoe box, dolls and doll clothes in another box, snap-lock beads in a tin can, lacing beads in another can, and so on.

**Classification and cooperation.**

Sorting toys is also an educational experience for children, and if you can put the right spin on it, a cooperative sort of game to play together.

*Approximate age range: 27 to 29 months*

# . . . A TOY STORAGE SYSTEM

In thinking through a storage system, consider fitting a closet with shelves for toys and games. If you don't want your child to be able to get into the closet, put a latch high up on the door. But there's no reason why your child shouldn't be able to get into the closet if you store lightweight and safe toys on the shelves he or she can reach.

**A bottom drawer.**

You can also store toys in a special bottom drawer of a desk or bureau. When you want to provide your child with the toys, pull out the entire drawer and set it on the floor.

**Cardboard file cabinets.**

A cardboard file cabinet is cheap, lightweight, safe, and can be taken on a trip.

*Approximate age range: 27 to 29 months*

155

# Don't Ask Questions Unless You Are Willing to Hear the Answer

Never ask your child a question unless you are prepared to hear your child's answer. For example, don't ask your child if she wants to kiss Grandma unless you are absolutely sure she or he will say yes. Keep this concept in mind throughout your years of child-rearing. For example, "Do you want to go to school?" is a risky question. A better question is, "What are you going to wear to school today?" And that only works if you don't impose a strict dress code.

*Approximate age range: 27 to 29 months*

# THE BIG NO

One way to get your indepence-loving, nay-saying toddler to say yes is to make a game of letting him or her say no until ready to say yes.

# HINT:

Don't start this game if you're in a hurry. And remember to give your child only those choices you're *absolutely* sure you can live with.

*Approximate age range: 27 to 29 months*

# PICTURE BOOKS FOR TWOS

Two-year-olds can handle books that are more complicated than baby books, but they still can't comprehend picture books with confusing, abstract pictures and overly complex stories. Select books for your child that have clear, recognizable pictures and a simple, memorable text.

**Great books for two-year-olds.**

In addition to the books listed on page 27, try some of these:

*Whose Mouse Are You?* by Robert Kraus
*Time for Bed* by Mem Fox
*Jesse Bear, What Will You Wear?* by Nancy White Carlstrom
*Where's My Baby?* by H. A. Rey
*Sleepy Book* by Charlotte Zolotow
*Mouse Around* by Pat Schories (Find the little mouse in every picture.)

**Rhyming books.**

Two-year-olds like rhythm and rhyme, as found in these books:

*Mother Goose*
*Jamberry* by Bruce Degen
*Polar Bear, Polar Bear, What Do You Hear?* by Bill Martin, Jr.
*Sheep in a Shop* by Nancy Shaw
*Not Now! Said the Cow* by Joanne Oppenheim
*Together* by George Ella Lyon

*Approximate age range: 27 to 29 months*

Art books and coffee table books may have big colorful pictures that your child might like to look at with you. But be aware that your child may want to touch the pictures and will see the pictures from a different point of view.

*Approximate age range: 27 to 29 months*

# LIGHTS, CAMERA, ACTION!

On sunny days when you have lots of energy and feel like planning a project with other parent friends and a bunch of toddlers, consider making a movie. Such projects can provide a focus to family gatherings. In future years at gatherings of the same people, you'll enjoy viewing the movie you made together. You need other gung-ho adults to help you, and, of course, you need a video camera. The plot of the movie can be as simple as "Let's Make a Parade." Take footage of each child getting ready for the parade (costumes, makeup, rehearsal) and then of the parade itself.

*Approximate age range: 27 to 29 months*

# BUSY WORK ON A RAINY DAY

Golden Paint with Water books are wonderful, mindless, *not* creative, *not* intellecutally stimulating but nevertheless captivating books for children. If they were the only art supplies you provided for your child, you would be amiss. But, assuming that is not the case, these books can keep a fussy child happy for a while. All you do is sit your child down in a comfortable place and provide a brush and water in a cup, preferably a bottom-weighted child's cup that doesn't easily tip. Your child paints the water onto the pictures, and presto, colors appear. Usually you can find these books in drugstore racks that also sell coloring books. Keep a supply handy for those times when you need to keep your child pleasantly occupied and can't think how to accomplish that.

*Approximate age range: 27 to 29 months*

# CHAPTER FIVE:
## 30 TO 35 MONTHS

As children pick up information about the world, they process it in two ways: through logical thinking and through fantasy.

**Logical thinking.**

Logical thinking is based on experience. In warm weather an ice cream cone melts. Sometimes it drips to the floor. When you get ice cream on your face, people wipe it off with a napkin. They get annoyed if ice cream drips on the floor. Thus, children slowly manage to learn—by applying logical thinking to experience—how to eat an ice cream cone neatly.

**Fantasy.**

Children are also able to make up stories and pictures in their minds. If you pick up a little pine cone and say to them, "Pretend this is a tickle monster, who is going to get you—now!" they will go along with you with glee, as long as you don't tickle them too hard. If you put a sock over your hand and say, "Meow," your toddler will pretend with you that your sock is a cat. Logical thinking and pretend thinking are both enjoyable for children.

*Approximate age range: 30 to 35 months*

**Children's fears.**

Children's ability to fantasize occasionally can get the best of some of them. Not all children suffer fearful fantasies, but some do imagine very scary scenarios, now and in the next few years. The fears of three- and four-year-olds can be worse because they have more knowledge with which to elaborate upon their scary feelings.

At this age, however, toddlers may be afraid of loud noises and unexpected sensations, such as people arriving at your house all of a sudden. They may be afraid of the doctor, of the toilet, of dogs, and of things they saw on television that they can't tell you about because they don't have the necessary language skills.

Without making too big a deal of your child's fears, listen to what you hear and respect your child's feelings. Offer comments, such as "That must have scared you." Cuddle your child when needed, waiting for your child to let go. Restrict television to appropriate shows, provide your child with a doll to "talk" to, and give your child many daily reasons to trust you and feel secure.

*Approximate age range: 30 to 35 months*

# UP AND DOWN STAIRS? NO SWEAT

Since children can walk upstairs and downstairs more easily now, you'll find it easier to take them places, such as a museum and the library. You can always use the public access ramps and elevators, of course, but children like to climb big sets of stairs with you. Sometimes going up and down the steps of an art museum is more fun than looking at the paintings inside. But be prepared to go slowly. Trying to hurry with a toddler in tow is pointless.

*Approximate age range: 30 to 35 months*

# INDEPENDENCE & SAFETY

Thirty-month-old children appreciate being able to do things for themselves, so when possible, let them. For example, they may like to have their own umbrella that is just their size. You have to watch constantly, however, for safety factors because children can't anticipate them. They don't know what problems an umbrella can cause. You do, so you explain and watch out.

*Approximate age range: 30 to 35 months*

# PLAY STRUCTURES

Toddlers this age crave suitable physical challenges. They love to visit parks that have climbing structures made just for children their age. Such structures usually have low ramps, slides, tunnels, and low platforms to play on.

**If you want to buy a jungle gym.**

If you are interested in building a jungle gym or helping your community build one, consult local nursery schools and day-care centers. Ask to see their catalogs for child-care equipment. Call the 800 numbers on the catalogs for information. Some companies sell climbing structures that parent volunteers can help put together for a community.

**If you want to build one.**

Consult woodworking books on children's furniture and play materials. You can find such books in libraries and bookstores. Some designs use tires as part of the structure. All climbing structures for toddlers should be safe, sturdy, stable, toppleproof, made of quality materials, and made with secure grab bars and handrails.

*Approximate age range: 30 to 35 months*

### Swings.

Baby swings that strap or hold toddlers in are still used by toddlers. In general, avoid swing sets made for older children. Toddlers are not old enough to comply with safety rules, such as "Don't ever walk in front of the swings." And they can't get up and out of the seats yet.

### Sandboxes.

Sand, like water, is a malleable material that children love. You don't have to build a fancy sandbox in the backyard, though you may enjoy doing so. If you're not a carpenter, just fill a toddler pool with sand. You can buy sand at gardening centers and stores that sell gravel and cement mix.

*Approximate age range: 30 to 35 months*

# Walking on a Balance Board

A balance board is a board lifted a few inches off the ground. Stepping up onto a balance board, walking across it, and stepping down provides toddlers with excellent exercise for their leg muscles and an opportunity to improve their sense of balance. To make a balance board put a 9-inch to 12-inch-wide board on two low boards or blocks. Make sure the balance board is safe and sturdy enough for your child to use. Supervise closely to make sure.

*Approximate age range: 30 to 35 months*

# TODDLER OBSTACLE COURSE

Set up an obstacle course for your toddler in an open grassy place. Some obstacles for your child to overcome might be: a tube to crawl through, a balance board, a tire to crawl over, and a small slide to climb up and slide down. If you like, set the objects up in a circle.

*Approximate age range: 30 to 35 months*

# MATCHING COLORS & DESIGNS

Help your child develop observation skills and learn words to describe colors and patterns by pointing out and discussing various designs found around the home. Your necktie collection may be of great interest to your child. You can go one step further by encouraging your child to see that certain designs and colors are the same and can be matched. Matching socks is also a good way to approach this activity and get a chore done at the same time.

*Approximate age range: 30 to 35 months*

# ARTISTS AT WORK

Here's an art project that produces a picture with texture that you can later describe with texture words, such as bumpy, rough, prickly, and sparkly. The project is a little messy so leave enough time—and be in the right mood.

1. Squeeze a small bottle of white glue over a piece of paper. You will have a "Jackson Polbck" glue painting. Or, pour the glue into a saucer and use a stick to dribble it on the paper.

2. Sprinkle the wet design with glitter, cornmeal, sugar, salt, rice, confetti, seeds, pine needles or sand.

The sprinkle WILL STICK to the GLUE... SEE?

STICK GLUE

3. Dump excess sprinkles into a storage container or the trash. If you dump it into a storage container, you can use it again.

4. Let the painting dry... and show it off.

MADE IT!

*Approximate age range: 30 to 35 months*

# A BUDDING GENIUS!

How can you tell if your child has a particular talent? Well, at this age, you can't. On the other hand, maybe you can. Look at it this way: Your child exhibits the universal talents of toddlers—a desire to learn and an absolute passion for experience.

*Approximate age range: 30 to 35 months*

# Drawing or Writing?

Continue to provide crayons and paper to draw with. Actually, there's no reason to assume that your child is always trying to draw a picture. Often, children are trying to write. They don't know what writing is, but they see you doing it; and because they like to copy you, they copy your writing actions. If you're perceptive you may see your child making shapes that look like letters from time to time. You don't need to teach your child to write at this point. That comes later. Most children learn to read and write when they are six. But if your child should ever ask how to draw a certain letter, demonstrate. Your child may or may not be able to copy you, but it's nice that he or she is interested. Some children like to pretend they are writing a book. Note that your toddler probably is able to hold a crayon more comfortably these days.

*Approximate age range: 30 to 35 months*

# WASHING HANDS . . .

Along with improved abilities to make art projects, toddlers have improved abilities to clean up afterward, too. They can help you wipe off a table with a damp sponge, and by now they can wash and dry their hands with minimal supervision. Inside, you may need to provide a stool for them to climb up to the sink, and you may have to mix the hot and cold water to make warm water. If you're outside gardening, you can give your child a bucket of sudsy water for washing up.

*Approximate age range: 30 to 35 months*

# . . . AND DRYING THEM

Children now are old enough to dry their own hands if you give them a small towel. They can learn to throw a paper towel away when they are done. They can learn to hang up a towel if the rack is low and easy for them to wrap a towel around. Some parents sew snaps or Velcro at the ends of towels so that they do not fall when used by a vigorous toddler.

*Approximate age range: 30 to 35 months*

# KNOW WHAT KIDS ARE CAPABLE OF

One pediatrician keeps a list posted in her office of all the things she has had to take out of kids' ears: toothpicks, crayons, beans, erasers, peanuts, and would you believe, a piece of salami? Be forewarned.

Watch your kid. How can you protect your child from all the hazards of the world? The answer is you can't. Too many things are out of your control. You just have to have faith that whatever happens you'll be strong enough to deal with it. But there are many hazards that are within your control. You can do something about them.

*Approximate age range: 30 to 35 months*

# AVOID KNOWN HAZARDS

Ask your pediatrician what to do if your child ingests poison. Know the procedure. Go over it with the people who take care of your child. Keep the poison control number posted. Program your phones so that the numbers for the ambulance, and the police and fire departments are easy to call. Post these numbers, too. Think ahead of time about how you would rescue your child and escape if your home were burning. Teach your child to stop at street corners. If your child will not comply, hold your child's hand.

*Approximate age range: 30 to 35 months*

# TRYING TO DRESS ONESELF

Children this age need still some help with dressing, but they like to do it themselves. So let them—if you have time. On weekends, for example, you can set out some clothes that are easy for your child to put on. Put the clothes on the floor; then sit and have a cup of coffee while your child works away at the task. Offer assistance only when requested. Be proud of your child's sartorial accomplishments.

**What to do when there's no time.**

Morning hassles can plague the parents of toddlers. Picture it: You have to get your child up and take him or her to the baby-sitter. You're dressed for work and ready for the day, but your toddler is cranky and uncooperative. What to do? Dress your fussy child. Don't get angry, just get the job done. Your toddler may not be happy, but that's life.

One alternative to difficult mornings: Ask the baby-sitter if you can deliver your child in pajamas. Some baby-sitters who care for children in their homes will allow this. Another alternative is to put your child to bed in the the next day's clothes. Sweatsuits, pajamas— what's the difference?

*Approximate age range: 30 to 35 months*

# DRESSING GAMES

**Find a red sock.**

Have your child look for items of clothing to wear, one by one. The reward for finding something is to put it on.

**This is the way we put on our shoes.**

To the tune of "Here We Go 'Round the Mulberry Bush," sing about the clothes you help your child put on:

*This is the way we put on our shoes,*
*Put on our shoes,*
*Put on our shoes,*
*This is the way we put on our shoes,*
*On a Monday morning.*

**One blue shirt and tickle you!**

After you put on an article of clothing, tickle your child. As you're dressing your child you say suspensefully, "One blue shirt . . . and tickle, tickle you!"

**How many clothes can you put on?**

This is a silly game for a day when you have nothing better to do.

*Approximate age range: 30 to 35 months*

# 5 Toddler Hit Songs

Jingle bells, jingle bells,
Jingle all the way;
Oh, what fun it is to ride
In a one-horse open sleigh, hey!
Jingle bells, jingle bells,
Jingle all the way;
Oh, what fun it is to ride
In a one-horse open sleigh, hey!

*Sing any time of year. Children like to
shake a little bell when they sing it.*

Twinkle, twinkle, little star,
How I wonder what you are.
Up above the world so high,
Like a diamond in the sky;
Twinkle, twinkle, little star,
How I wonder what you are.

I'm a little teapot,
Short and stout;
Here is my handle, *(put arm on hip)*
Here is my spout. *(bend other arm up)*
When I am all ready,
Then I shout,
Tip me over, *(bend to the side)*
And pour me out.

*Approximate age range: 30 to 35 months*

# Sing Them Together

If you're happy and you know it,
Clap your hands. *(clap, clap)*
If you're happy and you know it,
Clap your hands. *(clap, clap)*
If you're happy and you know it,
Then your face will surely show it,
If you're happy and you know it,
Clap your hands. *(clap, clap)*

*Clap as directed. Make up other verses with other actions: shake your head, touch your nose, jump up and down, stamp your feet, and so on.*

Row, row, row
Your boat,
Gently down the stream,
Merrily, merrily,
Merrily, merrily,
Life is but a dream.

*Imitate rowing motions with your arms, while sitting on the floor, as in a boat.*

*Approximate age range: 30 to 35 months*

# RHYTHM & RHYME

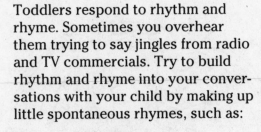

Toddlers respond to rhythm and rhyme. Sometimes you overhear them trying to say jingles from radio and TV commercials. Try to build rhythm and rhyme into your conversations with your child by making up little spontaneous rhymes, such as:

Hey, kid, whaddaya say?
How 'bout getting up today?

Here's what we are going to do:
Find the other purple shoe.

First the jacket, then the hat,
Next the mittens; that is that!

**Number rhymes.**

Numbers and letters are easy to rhyme with. Here are some very simple examples:

One, two,
Peek-a-boo!

One, two,
Tie the shoe!

A, B, C, D,
Can you see me?

One, two, three, four,
Have one bite and then some more!

*Approximate age range: 30 to 35 months*

# FINGER PLAY RHYMES

Finger play rhymes are rhymes you act out with your hands and fingers.
Children can't say them or do them as well as you can, but that doesn't bother
them. They love to try to imitate you, and sooner or later, they can. Here are
the words to two fingerplay rhymes, "Itsy Bitsy Spider" and "Two Little Blackbirds." Ask an older child to teach you and your child how to do them.

**"Itsy Bitsy Spider."***

Itsy Bitsy Spider went up the water spout,
Down came the rain, and washed the spider out.
Out came the sun,
And dried up all the rain,
And Itsy Bitsy Spider went up the spout again.

*Also known as
"Eentsy Weentsy Spider."

**"Two Little Blackbirds."**

Two little blackbirds
Sitting on a hill,
One named Jack,
One named Jill.
Fly away, Jack,
Fly away, Jill,
Come back, Jack,
Come back, Jill.

*Approximate age range: 30 to 35 months*

# TELEVISION AND TODDLERS

Many toddlers like to watch TV, and for short periods each day, watching TV can be a diversion. After an active afternoon of exploration and free play, for example, a child may enjoy watching a TV show for young children while you fix dinner. Often, tired parents at the end of a work day are relieved to have TV occupy their child while they are busy with household chores. And on weekend mornings you can sometimes get a little more needed sleep if your toddler will watch TV.

*Approximate age range: 30 to 35 months*

# How Does It Affect Them?

In time, children may turn into TV zombies, otherwise known as couch potatoes, if they watch too much TV. Remember that one of the main ways children
learn is by imitation. Children who watch shows that are too old for them and
too violent may want to imitate what they see. Another one of the main ways
that children learn is through concrete experience. TV is passive. While children are watching TV, they are not playing actively with materials that teach
them about the world. Fortunately, many toddlers don't really like TV that
much. Left to their own devices, they'll wander away and start playing with
toys. When that happens, turn the TV off. Don't have TV noise be a constant in
your child's auditory life.

*Approximate age range: 30 to 35 months*

# MY VOCABULARY GROWS . . .

**Verbs.**

If you say to your child, "What flies in the air?" your child will say, "Bird." If you ask, "What swims in the river?" your child will say, "Fish." Your child doesn't just suddenly comprehend these verbs at the age of 30 months. No, your child learns them because you teach them. The point is that at the age of 30 months your child is able to understand this kind of teaching. Your child has the potential to link certain animals with certain actions but needs your help to actualize the potential. After a while, you can play silly games with this knowledge. What does a fish do? Fly in the sky? Toddlers in the know find this great fun.

*Approximate age range: 30 to 35 months*

# . . . TO *450 WORDS!*

**Nouns.**

Not only does your child know the words to songs and rhymes, but your child is learning many new names for things. Your child may not be able to say them but will understand when you use names for articles of clothing, names for kitchen tools, names for different kinds of food, names for more animals, and the names of more people.

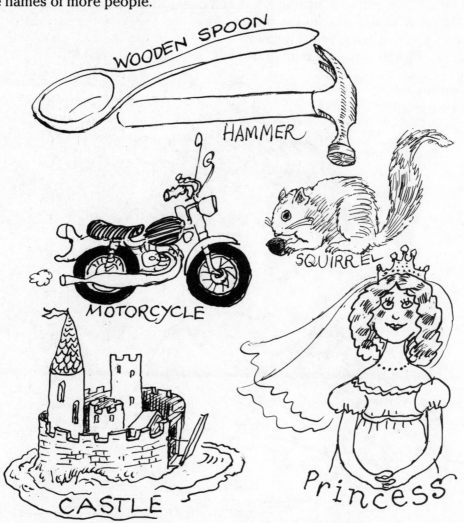

WOODEN SPOON

HAMMER

MOTORCYCLE

SQUIRREL

CASTLE

Princess

*Approximate age range: 30 to 35 months*

# COUNTING TO 5, 10, OR 20

Learning to count with you from 1 to 5, from 1 to 10, or even from 1 to 20 is a terrific verbal skill for toddlers to master. Your child doesn't understand the numbers. Counting is like chanting. Your toddler is learning the words to a chant, a perfectly appropriate activity for this age.

You can help your child learn to count by counting aloud together when you do things. When you walk upstairs, you can count them. When you put cans into the recycle bag, you can count them. When you pick up toys, you can count them, too. Children like to count things on their own. Don't worry if they don't do it correctly.

ONE...
TWO...
THREE...
FOUR...
FIVE!

*Approximate age range: 30 to 35 months*

# WHAT DO NUMBERS MEAN?

May I please have one block?

**The concept of one.**

Toddlers this age begin to understand the concept of "one." If your child is playing with blocks and you say, "Will you please give me one?" your child may be able to comply, daintily handing over just one.

**Other numbers.**

But toddlers don't know what other numbers mean. They can memorize numbers to count, and they understand the act of counting things, but the concept of numbers is beyond them for now. If your child counts something, say the peas on his or her plate, you can also count them—correctly, if you like. But don't try to explain why your count is correct; your toddler won't follow your logic—not yet. What you see is what they understand—the act of counting without the more sophisticated and more abstract level of knowledge to come.

*Approximate age range: 30 to 35 months*

# THE ALPHABET

Saying the alphabet, like counting, is equivalent to learning a chant. The letters of the alphabet are like the words to a song. And in fact the "Alphabet Song" is one of the songs young children like to sing best.

Letter recognition is another skill that you may see your toddler develop. Children may look at a gas station sign such as BP and say, "Look, Daddy, a B!" They are recognizing the shape of the letter, perhaps from watching a show such as *Sesame Street*. They don't yet understand how letters work, however. They are just recognizing them as they would recognize, say, a cow. This is not to diminish their accomplishment; on the contrary, be excited and say, "Yes, that's a B!"

*Approximate age range: 30 to 35 months*

# WHAT DO LETTERS MEAN?

That's a good question. What do letters mean? Children look at them on signs and on their cereal boxes. They stare at them as you read a book to them. Slowly, they may begin to sense a connection between the words you say and the letters on the box.

Eventually, with the help of grown-ups and older children who read to them and teach them, young children figure out the connection between letters and words. They learn to read around the age of six or seven. What toddlers need from you now is a print-rich environment in which they will see lots of letters and books, which you will gladly read to them. In this way the foundation for later reading is built.

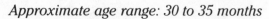

*Approximate age range: 30 to 35 months*

# GET DOWN ON THE FLOOR

Sometimes the best way to play with your child is to get down on the floor and do what your child is doing. Whatever the activity is, get into it from your child's point of view. Talk about it with your child. The words you use will enliven the experience for your child. Sometimes you can suggest a way to make an activity more exciting without really changing it. For example, if your child says, "I put my guy way up," you can say, "I put my guy way up too." Then you might add, "Where else can we put our guys?" thus expanding the activity to new places that can be described with more words.

*Approximate age range: 30 to 35 months*

# TALKING WITH OTHERS

You may hear your toddler talking in the other room and wonder who he or she is talking to. The answer may be a doll or teddy bear. Toddlers begin to invent dramatic play in this basic way. Don't interrupt. Just listen. Enjoy the experience as a reward for all the language you have taught your child.

*Approximate age range: 30 to 35 months*

# FEAR & FRUSTRATION

Children have all the feelings you have. They are afraid certain people will hurt them. They know what it feels like to be made fun of. They feel left out when they are the only young child in a group of older children who are ignoring them. They know what it feels like to be the most awkward child in a group or the slowest. They may not know the names for these feelings, but they have them, and you can tell, usually, when they are suffering simply by watching them. Sometimes all you have to do is go over and give them a little attention, a little assistance, and a little TLC.

*Approximate age range: 30 to 35 months*

# ANGER & RAGE

Sometimes it helps to understand that just as you get furious at your child, so does your child get furious with you. After all, you control every aspect of your child's life. When you are taking care of your child, you decide what your child will eat, where your child will play, and what will happen next. Your child is programmed to progress inexorably toward independence. The program may take 18 years to run its course, but the urge to experience more independence than you currently allow can send a child into a rage. WAA-A-A!!

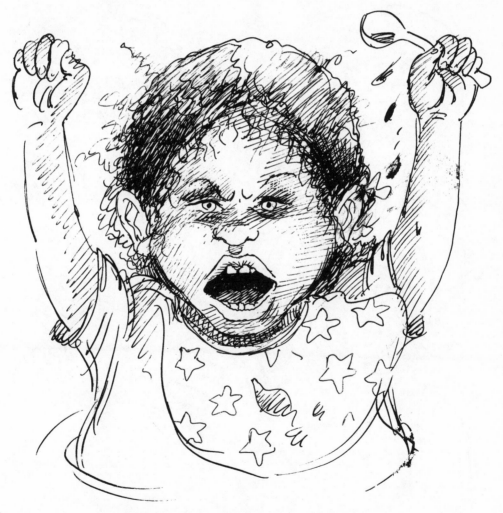

*Approximate age range: 30 to 35 months*

# SECURITY

You, your wife, and the other people who take care of your child are security to your child. You define the word with the care you provide: shelter, warmth, food, cleanliness, a healthful environment, language, and love. None of these items needs to have a high price tag attached to it. Your toddler doesn't care where he or she lives; all your toddler wants is a family in which people are there for one another.

*Approximate age range: 30 to 35 months*

# TRUST

Trust is developed in the early years of life. Children learn to trust people when people love them for themselves, are patient with them, and let them make mistakes. Children who learn to trust others develop a positive attitude about the outside world and want to learn more about it.

Grandparents can be wonderful caregivers because they seem to have the knack of providing uncritical love. They are patient, too, with children, having learned the folly of unimportant goals, such as being the best in the class. They value the important goals, such as feeling confident and being willing to take risks. If your child doesn't have grand-parents, consider adopting some in your community. Many senior citizens would like to have more contact with young children.

*Approximate age range: 30 to 35 months*

# CHAPTER SIX:
# *36 MONTHS (THREE YEARS)*

Every so often, it's healthy to stop and analyze how your family's daily systems are working for every family member. Ask yourself, for example, which family systems are working for your toddler? Which ones don't work? Which could be improved? Eliminated? Your child is too little to participate in a family meeting, but such meetings are a good idea. Establish the concept now, and someday your child will be able to contribute.

**Three-year-olds need families that function effectively.**

No family functions effectively all of the time, but your family should function fairly well most of the time. If not, deal constructively with the situation. At your family meeting, you and your wife may want to include older siblings and a baby-sitter who cares for your child on a daily basis. Focus on particular problems, not people. For example, on discipline. Or mealtimes. On mornings. On bedtime. On upcoming holidays. Talk about the problems without blaming people.

**Identify specific problems.**

Encourage everyone to share feelings about a particular problem.

**Consider and evaluate solutions.**

Encourage everyone to brainstorm a variety of solutions. Weigh the advantages and disadvantages of each.

**Choose a solution that everyone is willing to try. Set a trial period.**

Try it for the length of the trial period. Invite everyone to meet again.

**Reevaluate at the end of the trial period.**

If the solution worked, great. If not, try another one. These meetings do not have to be formal; they can take place casually at mealtime.

*Approximate age: 36 months*

**Three-year-olds love rituals.**

Rituals, such as family meals, holiday celebrations, and birthday parties, are important to children at this age. Rituals help children get a sense of the rhythm of the year and learn how to participate in family traditions. If you have special traditions you want your child to learn, be a part of making them happen. Discuss ideas at family meetings. Don't leave everything up to your wife. If you don't like the rituals you grew up with, think creatively as a family about establishing new ones.

*Approximate age: 36 months*

# CELEBRATING A THIRD BIRTHDAY

As with all celebrations that you want toddlers to enjoy, don't make your plans too lavish. Think back. Do you remember your third birthday party? Hardly anyone does. So, instead of trying to make the most memorable party ever, concentrate on the tried-and-true pleasures of life. Food: Serve ice cream cones first and then cupcakes. Serve small cans or boxes of apple juice. Sit in a circle and play finger play games with the children. Ask them which ones to play. Sing songs with them; again, asking for requests. Roll a ball back and forth, and then go on a follow-the-leader march. For treats to send home, you might give out animal crackers, toy horns, and party hats.

*Approximate age: 36 months*

Approximate age: 36 months

# RIDING TOYS WITH PEDALS

Most three-year-olds can learn to pedal tricycles by themselves. But tricycles today come in different sizes and shapes. Some are just too big for three-year-olds to handle. If you are going to buy one for your child, have your child try out different vehicles in the store before deciding which one to purchase. You can also ask other children on the playground to let your child try out their trikes. Watch for trikes at tag sales; often you can get good ones very inexpensively this way.

**Safety precautions:**

1. Check the trike carefully to make sure that it is in good working order.

2. Explain very clearly to your child where the trike may and may not be ridden.

3. Observe your child closely to make sure the rules are being followed. If not, take the trike away for a few days.

4. Show your child where to put the trike at the end of the day.

*Approximate age: 36 months*

# CONSTRUCTION VEHICLES

Good sturdy construction trucks that work with real sand and dirt give children hours of outside pleasure. They like to pretend with these vehicles that they are grown-ups building things. Toy wheelbarrows are also appreciated for transporting dirt, stones, dolls, and other toys around. The next time you pass a construction site with your child, stop and look together at what's happening. You may see your child later imitate through play some of the workers.

*Approximate age: 36 months*

# ROUGH & TUMBLE PLAY

Many dads like to roughhouse with their children, who delight in this kind of play as long as you are not too rough and you stop when they want you to. Roughhousing with toddlers should not really be rough at all. It's just a matter of your lifting them up, swinging them down, twirling them around, and so forth—always safely and with their enjoyment clear.

**The 2 worst times for roughhousing:**

1. Before meals

2. Before bed

If you roughhouse with a child before meals, your child will not eat. If you roughhouse before bedtime, your child will not sleep. Think about it.

*Approximate age: 36 months*

# TIME OUT

Time Out refers to the practice of separating a child from a situation in which he or she is misbehaving. It is somewhat similar to Going to Your Room. Telling a child to "go to your room" is generally an angrier admonition than telling a child to take time out. A child sent to his or her room feels banished; while a child sent to sit on a certain chair and take time out is being given a chance to rest and get a grip on his or her behavior. Time Out lasts for five or ten minutes; it doesn't need to be long. If the Time Out child falls asleep, then you know what the problem was.

*Approximate age: 36 months*

# MAKING PRESENTS

Young children can put their artistic talents to use by making things to give to people as presents. Toddlers are not yet skilled in all the arts, but they can make a few things quite decently.

**Bead necklaces.**

See page 101 for information on beads. When children are younger, you have to help them string beads. Most three-year-olds are now able to string four beads by themselves. As your child gives away bead necklaces, replenish the supply of beads and strings.

**Bouquets of flowers.**

Save flower baskets from floral arrangements. Throw away the dead flowers and dry out the green spongy thing inside. When your child is ready to make a bouquet, wet the sponge thoroughly. Supply your child with flowers that have sturdy stems. Your child can stick them into the green sponge and make a beautiful bouquet.

**Drawings.**

Keep an assortment of inexpensive plastic frames on hand to display your child's drawings for gifts.

*Approximate age: 36 months*

# GIVING PRESENTS

It's nice to offer your child the opportunity to give homemade presents to people. Grandparents love to receive presents from their grandchildren; this is one way to pay them back for their help. But there are others, too, who appreciate a kind gesture from a child: teachers, librarians, parents of newborns, and new children in the neighborhood. By giving gifts, children can learn at an early age the rewards of generosity.

*Approximate age: 36 months*

# BUILDING A BRIDGE FROM BLOCKS

Show your child how to build a simple bridge with blocks. First, put two blocks down, separated by a little space. Then put another block on top. Describe what you are doing, concluding, "And that makes a bridge. Can you build one like it?" Your child is probably old enough now to understand what you did, to remember it, and to now be able to build a bridge like yours.

In the same way, you can show your child how to build other structures, such as a little house—perhaps with a square block and a triangle roof. Don't get too complicated. Pay attention to what your child can and can't do. Offer only enough suggestions to make things interesting, not discouraging.

*Approximate age: 36 months*

# BLOCKS LAST A LONG TIME

While your child may not be able to make complex structures with blocks now, your child will grow more adept as time goes on. Blocks are expensive, but they are a good investment because they lend themselves to creative expression and logical thinking. Block play can last well into second grade and beyond.

Blocks enable children to represent the world around them. As children grow, they represent the world with more complexity. For example, a kindergartener who visits the zoo can come home and build a zoo with blocks. To encourage the benefits that blocks provide, help your child play with them. When your child builds an especially interesting block structure, leave it up for a while. Take a picture of it with your child in the picture. Start a photo gallery on the refrigerator to display the block structures your child makes.

*Approximate age: 36 months*

# TAKING TURNS

Learning to share and take turns is one of the most important achievements of childhood. It does not come easily, but the process of learning to share begins when children are toddlers. Three-year-olds are capable of waiting in line for a snack if the line isn't too long, and they are capable of waiting for a toy or their turn in a game if the wait isn't too long.

*Approximate age: 36 months*

# LITTLE BRATS

Sometimes as a parent you may have the experience of watching your child wait valiantly for his or her turn to come, only to be stymied by a perfectly wretched little brat who will not give up what your child has been waiting for. What can you do?

You can try to talk the bratty child out of the toy, perhaps by offering something else that is quite desirable. You can take the role of enforcer by taking the toy away from the brat and saying, "It's not your turn any longer. Come, I'll help you find something else to enjoy." If the bratty child proves to be utterly intransigent, you might just want to take your child and go off to another part of the playground or playroom.

Be a little sympathetic toward the wretch who has spurned your child, however, because another day that child could be your child. Rare is the toddler who doesn't get selfish from time to time.

*Approximate age: 36 months*

# FEEDING MYSELF RATHER NICELY

Todders have come a long way as far as feeding themselves. They are now skilled at using both forks and spoons, they can drink from a cup, they can sip from a straw, and they can eat a Popsicle. They can even take a napkin and wipe their mouths.

*Approximate age: 36 months*

# GOING TO RESTAURANTS

Three-year-olds are not the world's worst dinner companions. They can sit up in a high chair and eat properly. They like to look at the other people in a restaurant. They seem to enjoy the restaurant scene and often are cute enough to receive special attention from waiters and waitresses.

But don't make the mistake of going to a fancy, expensive restaurant with a three-year-old. Unless the restaurant has fallen on hard times, you won't be welcome, and the restaurant probably won't have a nice, comfortable, safe, and clean high chair for your child. Fast-food restaurants, such as McDonald's and Burger King, accommodate children easily. Italian, Mexican, and Chinese restaurants are usually friendly to toddlers, too, but don't go when your child is tired and whiny, and do bring along a few little toys.

*Approximate age: 36 months*

# UNDERSTANDING EXPLANATIONS

WHEN I GO
TO WORK
I THINK OF YOU
AND LOVE YOU
ALL DAY LONG!

Three-year-olds can understand reasonable explanations, so tell them in simple terms where you go when you go to work and that, indeed, you love them all day long. Don't apologize for working. Explain, again in simple terms, that you have to work so that you will have money to buy food and clothes and toys. Don't ask, "Can I go to work now?" That's not up to your child. Instead, say, "I'm going to work now, and I'll think of you all day long."

*Approximate age: 36 months*

# COOPERATION

Children can be impossible in grocery stores, there's no doubt about it. However, they can also be helpful, especially if you encourage this trait. Let them reach out and grab certain things, but set limits on this behavior. For example, when you enter the store, you can say, "When we find your snack, you can carry it." Then let your child look for it, and when you find it, carry it.

*Approximate age: 36 months*

# CUTTING WITH SCISSORS

Three-year-olds can begin to learn how to cut little pieces of paper with scissors. You can help them by placing your hand over your child's hand and then cutting. Your child can't use grown-up scissors; they are too big. You need to get a pair of small children's scissors. You can buy them in pharmacies and craft stores. Children's scissors have blunted ends for safety. Right from the beginning, teach your child never to run with scissors and to put them away in a special place when finished.

*Approximate age: 36 months*

# MY FIRST & LAST NAME

Children can now learn to say both their first and last name in response to the question, "What's your name?" You can show your child how to write his or her initials or name, too. Sometimes children can learn to recognize their name, if it's short, not by reading it but by memorizing the shapes the letters make.

*Approximate age: 36 months*

# PLAYING BABY

As children grow, they seem to take two steps forward and one step backward. Sometimes they act so babyish you wonder what's wrong. Nothing's wrong. They're just making a nostalgic trip back to babyhood. Maybe they need a little more of the kind of cuddling they remember getting when they were babies and that they see other babies getting. Don't be concerned when your child acts this way. We all do it from time to time.

*Approximate age: 36 months*

# PLAYING GROWN-UP

Other times, your three-year-old will seem to work at a job like a grown-up, especially if you are nearby, occasionally helping and offering praise. Children like independence as well as dependence, and you need to supply opportunities for them to experience both. Gradually as they grow, they become more and more independent. This kind of back-and-forth progress is natural.

*Approximate age: 36 months*

# MY VOCABULARY GROWS TO *1,000 WORDS!*

Of all the things that toddlers learn, language is the most remarkable. Think of it: At age one a child can say only two or three words, but at age three the same child understands up to a thousand words. A three-year-old can use words to ask questions, give explanations, describe things, express feelings, greet people, fantasize, and sing.

But knowing many words does not necessarily give children the ability to communicate. They have to learn to pronounce them, to make mistakes, to construct sentences that get more and more elaborate, and to listen.

Young children have to *want* to use words, *want* to talk, and feel that others *want* to talk with them. That's where you come in. By continuing to talk with your child, you convey on an ongoing basis the sense that communication between people is a vital part of life.

*Approximate age: 36 months*

# COMMUNICATION & FRIENDSHIP

Your child is now able to tell you about things that have happened to him or her. The accounts may be halting and inarticulate, but listen. And comment. Sometimes all you have to do is say back what your child is saying to show you understand.

If you are away from home on a trip, take time to talk to your child on the phone. Be patient because your child may not be able to say much on the phone. The open and friendly communication patterns that you establish now will serve you well in 20 years when you two drop your parent/child roles and become good friends.

HI!

*Approximate age: 36 months*

# STORYTELLING

Children like to listen to stories that you read to them and that they hear on tape. Sometimes they want to tell these stories back to you, and they can do this surprisingly well, especially if you know the story and help them along. From time to time, listen to your child's favorite stories on tape in the car. That way you'll both know the same stories.

"AND DEN TROLL SAID, "WHO DAT TRAMP OVER ME BRIDGE?"

*Approximate age: 36 months*

# LEARNING HOW TO BEHAVE

In general, three-year-olds are a bit more civilized than two-year-olds. They like to behave properly, but often don't know how. When you take your child into a new situation, explain how people will act and what you expect. For example, you might say the first time you take the train together, "People on the train like to be quiet because they are tired. So we will read together quietly. When we get home, I will read a book to you out loud." Your child will be able to look at books quietly only for a short while, so you need to have other things for him or her to play with on the train, too.

*Approximate age: 36 months*

# A STRONG DESIRE TO LEARN

Since toddlers learn by doing, you have to keep a close eye on them to make sure that their explorations and activities don't get them into trouble. This may seem like a lot of work, but letting them loose is worse and far more dangerous.

*Approximate age: 36 months*

# How to Teach a Toddler

The home is the child's first school, and you are one of your child's first teachers, but that doesn't mean that you need to be a strict schoolmaster. The kind of education that is needed in the home is a gentle, joyous, and casual kind of education that goes on as naturally as conversation and play. For that is precisely it: conversation and play are the two main ingredients of high-quality education for toddlers.

**Four tips for teaching toddlers effectively.**

**1. Watch.**

To teach your child in the best way, you must first learn to identify and support your child's investigations. Observe your child to see what he or she is interested in at the moment. Whatever it is, allow your child to find out more about it, provided the investigatons are safe—for your child, other people, and your home.

**2. Talk.**

Talk about whatever it is that interests your child. Name it, describe it, ask questions. Talk with your child, not at him or her. Don't overdo it. Try to guess what your child would like you to say or tell about. If you think he or she would like you to be quiet, be quiet.

**3. Introduce new experiences at the right moment.**

If your child is absorbed in watching the cat, don't distract him or her by calling attention to a new ball. Wait until an appropriate moment comes.

**4. Don't be pushy.**

Enjoy your child and your child's interests. Don't insist that your child be interested in something else, for your sake. On the contrary, try to interest yourself in your child's interests, for your child's sake. If you feel bored with your child's interests, try to see them through your child's eyes, not your own. Assuming the perspective of a child can be a mind-opening and very stimulating experience.

*Approximate age: 36 months*

# SELF-ESTEEM

EVEN WHEN I'M MAD AT YOU, I LOVE — YOU!

Your self-esteem affects your child's self-esteem. What you feel about yourself is an important part of what you convey each day to your child about people and life. The more you feel a sense of your own worth, the less apt you will be to use your child to compete for you and make you happy.

**Don't neglect yourself.**

As you take care of your child's emotional, physical, and educational growth, take care of those parts of yourself, too. Give yourself rights as a person: even the right to resent being a parent sometimes. Give your wife those rights, too.

*Approximate age: 36 months*

# COMPASSION FOR OTHERS

Children imitate grown-ups. Those lucky children who regularly see grown-ups comforting children and each other are bound sooner or later to imitate that behavior. That's why it is not unusual to see todders express compassion toward one another. One child cries, and another comes over to give a hug. When you see this, you know you're doing a good job as a parent.

*Approximate age: 36 months*

# ART, FANTASY & REALITY

Young children live in two worlds: the world of fantasy, in which monsters and princesses can scare them and reassure them, and the world of reality, in which real people can scare them and reassure them. Separating the two worlds is one of the tasks of childhood, and it takes many years. Usually by the time children are seven or eight, they are able to do so with confidence.

But before that, children live in both worlds, and that makes life both confusing and wonderfully rich for them. Literature, art, dance, and music are, as always, among the best ways for children to experience both fantasy and reality. Children don't need lessons in these areas as much as they need time, good art materials, space to dance and move in, and creative adults who sympathize with their artistic and scientific explorations. Be one of those people for your child, and let your child's imagination bring back to you some of the enchantment of childhood.

*Approximate age: 36 months*

# PICTURE BOOKS FOR THREES

The following are a little more complex but not necessarily better than old favorites that children continue to love. The books in this list will last for years, too.

*Ask Mr. Bear* by Marjorie Flack
*The Golden Egg Book* by Margaret Wise Brown
*The Runaway Bunny* by Margaret Wise Brown
*The Noisy Books* by Margaret Wise Brown
*Big Joe's Trailer Truck* by Joseph Mathieu
*Is Your Mama a Llama?* by Steven Kellogg
*The Little Engine That Could* by Watty Piper
*Arrow to the Sun* by Gerald McDermott
*The Snowy Day* by Ezra Jack Keats
*Where the Wild Things Are* by Maurice Sendak
*Wheels on the Bus* by Paul Zelinsky
*Curious George* by H. A. Rey
*Caps for Sale* by Esphyr Slobodkina
*The Storybook Prince* by Joanne Oppenheim
*If You Give a Mouse a Cookie* by Laura J. Numeroff
*The Tale of Peter Rabbit* by Beatrix Potter
*Pretend You're a Cat* by Jean Marzollo
*Potluck* by Anne Shelby

*Approximate age: 36 months*

# CONGRATULATIONS!

Congratuations on being a father of a three-year-old child. Think back to your three-year-old as a brand-new infant, and marvel at how far your child has come. Your ballet dancer may be able to balance on one foot for about two seconds. Bravo!

Your three-year-old also may be able to kick a ball about 10 feet. Hooray! Your child may enjoy playing with other children and like learning from them. Yes! All of which gives you immense joy and a feeling of unbounded pride, which you can share with other parents of threes who undoubtedly feel exactly the same way.

*Approximate age: 36 months*

# You're the Father of a Three-year-old

Think back three years ago to yourself as a new father, and marvel at how far you've come, too. That's three long years of parenting, during which time you have developed skills you probably never knew you had within you to learn. There is no one style of parenting that works better than all others, provided that love and consistency are part of the overall approach. You have developed your style, and it fits your child just right.

*Approximate age: 36 months*

# WHAT NOT TO EXPECT

Don't expect your three-year-old to be all grown up. Parents who dreaded the terrible twos are sometimes disappointed in the so-called better threes. Three-year-olds can be like two-year-olds—often. Threes still like to make play dough. Sorry, but they are not ready yet for French cooking.

*Approximate age: 36 months*

# WHAT TO EXPECT

Expect three-year-olds to continue to be active investigators of life. Expect them to express their feelings much of the time, and to enjoy playing with familiar children and interested adults. If you worry that your child is too passive, too uninterested in others, and too reluctant to verbalize feelings, you may want to ask your pediatrician or the local public elementary school administrator for information on programs to help preschoolers with learning disabilities, specific and identifiable neurological or emotional problems. Some three-year-olds have physical handicaps, such as deafness or blindness, that can impair their progress. Many cities and towns have wonderful special programs for children with special needs.

Most of all, expect your child to be your child—nobody else's and nobody else. Expect that your love for your child will continue to grow and grow.

*Approximate age: 36 months*

# MORE ABOUT THE AUTHOR

Jean Marzollo is the author of many books for children, including *Pretend You're a Cat, Close Your Eyes, Ten Cats Have Hats, In 1492, In 1776, The Teddy Bear Book*, and the I Spy series. For 20 years she was the editor of Scholastic's *Let's Find Out* early childhood magazine. She has written about parenting in *Parents* magazine, *Working Mother*, and *Family Circle.* She is a graduate of the University of Connecticut and the Harvard Graduate School of Education. She lives with her family in Cold Spring, New York.

# MORE ABOUT THE ILLUSTRATOR

Irene Trivas is the author and illustrator of several children's books, including *Annie . . . Anya: A Month in Moscow* and *Emma's Christmas.* She has illustrated many other children's books, such as *Potluck, The Pain and the Great One, My Mother's House, My Father's House, Who'll Pick Me Up When I Fall?* and *The One in the Middle Is a Green Kangaroo.* Before she began to illustrate picture books, she had a successful career as an animation designer and director. She is a graduate of UCLA and lives in South Ryegate, Vermont.